THE MAKING OF THE ENGLISH BIBLE

THE MAKING *of the* ENGLISH BIBLE

With an
Introductory Essay on the Influence
of the English Bible on
English Literature

By the
REV. SAMUEL McCOMB, M.A., D.D.

Emmanuel Church, Boston
Formerly Professor of Church History at
Queen's University, Canada

41892

NEW YORK
MOFFAT, YARD AND COMPANY
1909

TO
THE MEMORY OF

MY MOTHER

CONTENTS

CHAPTER   PAGE

     PREFATORY NOTE vii

     INTRODUCTION ix

I   WILLIAM TINDALE—THE FATHER OF THE ENGLISH BIBLE 1

II THE CONTRIBUTION OF MILES COVERDALE . 27

III THE CONTRIBUTION OF THE GENEVAN VERSION 40

IV THE CONTRIBUTION OF THE BISHOPS' BIBLE 54

V THE ROMAN CATHOLIC CONTRIBUTION . . 63

VI THE CONTRIBUTION OF THE AUTHORISED VERSION 87

VII THE CONTRIBUTION OF THE ANGLO-AMERICAN VERSION 100

APPENDIX:

  Note A—The English Bible before Tindale . 129

  Note B—Tindale's Debt to the Wycliffite Versions 135

  Note C—On the Origin and History of the Latin Vulgate 141

  Note D—Wrong or Inadequate Renderings in the Vulgate 155

  Note—The Greek of the New Testament . . 162

BIBLIOGRAPHY 167

  Table I . . . . . Facing Page 170

  Table II . . . . . " " 180

INDEX 185

PREFATORY NOTE

In the following pages an attempt is made to indicate the sources of the English Bible and to estimate the literary influences that have conspired to make it the most venerable of our classics. The history of its external fortunes has been recently told with knowledge and ability by Mr. H. W. Hoare in his *Evolution of the English Bible,* and for the first time its great obligations to the Roman Catholic English Version have been fully illustrated by Dr. J. G. Carleton in his *The Part of Rheims in the Making of the English Bible.* Dr. Lupton's general account of the English Versions in Hastings' *Dictionary of the Bible* (extra volume) is scholarly and abreast of our latest information. To these writers I desire to express my acknowledgments. My especial thanks are due to Professor J. H. Gardiner of Harvard University, for his kindness in making several valuable suggestions.

BOSTON, *May*, 1909,

INTRODUCTION

THE belief that the Bible is the monumental record of a Divine revelation, the supreme witness to the reality of God and of the moral order of the world, constitutes its primary and essential value as an appeal to our ethical and religious needs. Modern criticism has indeed made an end of the notion—a survival of Protestant scholasticism—of its merely verbal inspiration and authority, but with the destruction of the letter has come the emancipation of the spirit. The Bible is no longer a consecrated idol. It has become the spiritual servant of humanity and has entered on a fresh career of power and permanence. In English-speaking countries, at least, its spiritual force is unabated, though its coercive authority has gone. Thousands of men and women to-day are studying the Bible with joy in the light shed by the new knowl-

edge of our time and are finding in it, as
their fathers found, the source of a truly
spiritual ideal of life and the unquenched
fuel that kindles imagination and feeds the
fire of moral affections.   And perhaps the
best witness to the truth of this assertion is
the slow but sure progress in popular favour
which the Revised Version is making in its
two slightly divergent forms, the English and
the American editions; for the popular demand is for a version which, at whatever sacrifice, will give clearest and purest expression
to the sense of the original documents.   To
the literary critic, indeed, who is more con-
cerned with the form than the idea, the revision may well seem "an elaborately foolish
attempt "[1] to improve upon the most venerable of English classics; but after all, the popular instinct is sound. No æsthetic attrac-
tions, no pedigree, however honourable, can
bear out the application of the crucial and
final test of faithfulness to the primitive
texts. The average reader of the Bible in

[1] Saintsbury, *Short History of English Literature*, p. 380.

our day asks that these old Greek and
Hebrew writings should speak to him as they
spoke to their first readers, freed from the
meanings imposed upon them by later ages
and from the unconscious errors of imperfect
scholarship. A Bible that refuses to meet
this demand may serve the needs of a coterie;
it cannot speak home to a wider humanity.
On the other hand, a translation which would
break away from the past and pedantically
renounce the moving and living rhythm of
earlier workers would make no wide appeal
to the popular mind. Having no root in the
soil of a great literary tradition it would soon
wither away.

The purpose of this book is not to give a
history of the English Bible, but to indicate
in the light of recent investigations the immense debt our latest revision owes to its
predecessors, and to estimate the contribu-
tions to it from the most diverse sources. It
will appear that our Bible is the most catholic
thing in all literature. Friend and foe alike
have been pressed into its service. Men of

every type of religious conviction have, directly or indirectly, willingly or unwillingly, left their mark upon its pages. Reformer and Humanist, Roman Catholic and Protestant, Prelatist and Puritan, Calvinist and Arminian, Trinitarian and Unitarian, Orthodox and Liberal—all meet here if nowhere else and lose their mutual discords in a higher symphony. It is this interesting fact that we propose to investigate in these pages.

CHAPTER I

WILLIAM TINDALE—THE FATHER OF THE ENGLISH BIBLE

THE Father of the English Bible as we have it is William Tindale, a man whose history, as Froude [1] remarks, is lost in his work and whose epitaph is the Reformation. His parentage, the date and place of his birth, are not certainly known. Recent investigation, however, points to the parish of Slymbridge in the English county of Gloucester as his birthplace, and to 1495 as about the time he was born. [2] Foxe, the Martyrologist, and our only authority for Tindale's early life, tells us, " He was brought up from a child in the University of Oxford, where he grew and increased as well in the knowledge of tongues and other liberal arts as especially in the knowledge of the Scriptures, whereunto his mind was singularly ad-

[1] *History of England*, Vol. II, p. 40.
[2] See Demaus, *William Tindale* (2d edition), pp. 22, 23.

dicted.'' It is probable that Colet had left Oxford to become the famous London preacher when Tindale entered the University, but the future translator of the Bible must have felt the stir created by the great Dean's famous lectures on the Epistles of St. Paul, when for the first time Englishmen felt the vital breath of the Apostolic teaching and realised, as has been finely said, that '' Greece had risen from the dead with the New Testament in her hand.''

After graduation he proceeded to Cambridge, where Erasmus had taught Greek and put life into the dry bones of the deadest of dead divinity. It was while here that the great Humanist's Greek Testament with a Latin translation, which marks an epoch in religious history, must have fallen into his hands and lit the fire of a sacred ambition that death alone could quench. If we call Tindale the Father of the English New Testament, we may fitly term Erasmus its grandfather. The work of Erasmus, published in 1516, was an appeal by a son of the Church,

dedicated to the Pope and addressed to all
thoughtful and cultivated men. Disregard-
ing traditional interpretation, throwing over-
board the allegorical method that throughout
the Middle Ages had substituted sound for
sense, he sought to get at the real meaning
of the sacred writers, the exact teaching of
Christ and His Apostles. It was this Græco-
Latin edition that broke the traditional in-
fallibility of the Vulgate. What Erasmus
achieved for the scholar, Tindale would do
for the poor and the illiterate. The pupil
had imbibed the spirit of his master's words
—" I wish that they—the Gospels and
Epistles—were translated into all languages
so as to be read and understood not only by
Scots and Irishmen, but even by Saracens
and Turks." [1] Like Wycliffe before him,
Tindale came to believe that the Bible was
not, as the mediæval mind supposed, the
peculiar property of ecclesiastics and theologians, but rather the people's book; not a
part of a deposit which the Church held in

[1] *Exhortation*, prefixed to the Greek New Testament, 1516.

trust for the laity and which it dispensed in
fragments and these fragments veiled beneath a traditional gloss, but a book open to
all men, for all, to be understood of all.   This
belief marks the uprise of the democratic
spirit in religion.   Though ordained to the
priesthood, there is no trustworthy evidence
that Tindale assumed monastic vows. It was
while under a patron's roof in his native
county that he made, by way of rejoinder to
a theological opponent, his famous boast:
" If God spare my life, ere many years I will
cause a boy that driveth the plough to know
more of the Scripture than thou doest." [1]

In 1523 he went up to London to interest
the Bishop of that city in his projected translation.   His hopes were doomed to disap-
pointment.   Bishop Tunstall, who though a
friend of the New Learning was hostile to
the Reformation, gave him no encourage-
ment, and the conviction was forced upon
him that " not only was there no room in my
Lord of London's palace to translate the

[1] Foxe, *Acts and Monuments*, Vol. V, p. 117.

New Testament," but also that there was no place to do it in all England.[1] Henceforth, like Dante, he was to prove—

> "How salt the savor is of others' bread,
> How hard the passage to descend and climb
> By others' stairs." [2]

Illegal as it was to print the Scriptures without episcopal sanction, he realised that if the task to which he felt himself called was to be done, it could be done only on the Continent. In the spring of 1524 he left England for Germany, never to return. Early the following year, we find him busy at Cologne superintending the printing of his translation of the New Testament. Compelled to flee before the work was finished, he found a refuge in Worms, a centre of the new opinions, where he issued two editions, which in due time, to the number of six thousand copies, were secretly smuggled into England, and as secretly sold in town and country. In 1530 he published the Pentateuch in English from the original Hebrew, to be fol-

[1] *Preface to the Pentateuch.*
[2] *Paradiso* XVII. (Plumptre's translation.)

lowed by the Book of Jonah a year later.   In 1534 [1] a revised edition of the New Testament and the Pentateuch appeared.   In May of 1535 he was betrayed by a false friend, arrested, thrown into prison at Vilvorde near Brussels, and on October 6, 1536, he crowned a life of self-denial, of devotion and scholarly simplicity, with a martyr's death.

As has been said, Tindale was not the first to render the New Testament in English. [2] Two centuries before his day, Wycliffe and his disciples had given the Bible to the people and had thereby stirred a religious ferment which had not wholly died away even in Tindale's time.   But in the England of the fourteenth century, Hebrew and Greek were unknown, and the Wycliffite translation was made, not from the originals, but from the current traditional and rather corrupt text of the Latin Vulgate.   It is the peculiar

[1] Two other editions appeared during Tindale's lifetime, one dated 1535, and the other 1535, 1534.   This latter is the text Rogers took over and embodied in Matthew's Bible of 1537.   It embodies Tindale's last corrections.   The 1535 edition is probably a pirated misprint.

[2] See Appendix, Note A.

glory of Tindale that he was the first to go
behind the Latin Bible to the fountain head
and render directly the original documents.
His design was to translate the entire
Bible, but his taking off by his enemies
in 1536 prevented its complete accomplish-
ment. We owe to him, first, the New Testament; second, the Pentateuch; third, according to an old tradition, from Joshua to II
Chronicles, inclusive. This last portion he
is believed to have left behind in manuscript
in the hands of his friend, John Rogers, who
afterwards embodied it in Matthew's Bible.
This tradition has been to some extent cor-
roborated by a passage in Hall's *Chronicle*
(1548), in which, under the twenty-seventh
year of King Henry VIII, we read: " This
man [Tindale] translated the New Testament
into English and first put it in print, and
likewise he translated the five books of
Moses, Joshua, Judges, Ruth, the Books of
the Kings, and the Books of Paralipomenon,
Nehemiah or the First of Esdras, the
Prophet Jonas, and no more of the Holy

Scriptures."[1] Tindale probably completed
the historical books of the Old Testament,
ending with II Chronicles, and it was this
completed portion which was afterwards
incorporated in Matthew's Bible.

Tindale has himself told us the motives
that lay behind his work and the causes that
induced him to undertake it. He lays em-
phasis on the failure of the clergy as a teaching body. As a chaplain tutor in the house
of one of the landed gentry, he met " abbots,
deans, archdeacons, with divers other divines," with whom he disputed, " laying
plainly before them the open and manifest
places of Scripture." These theologians
revealed an appalling ignorance of Biblical
commonplaces, and what they did know was
obscured by rules of interpretation that could
not stand the light of a world on which the
Renaissance had dawned.[2]   The sense of

[1] See Westcott, *History of the English Bible*, 3rd edition,
p. 172.

[2] We have independent evidence of the deplorable ignorance of the clergy in Tindale's native shire in the sixteenth
century. Bishop Hooper, some thirty years later than

the Divine word was obscured by expositions " clean contrary unto the process, order, and meaning of the text—which
thing only moved me to translate the New
Testament."[1] His version was born of pity
for the spiritual needs of his countrymen.
To the charge that he was moved to translate
the Bible in order to support the claims of a
sect, his own words are a sufficient reply:
" I take God to witness," he says, " to record
to my conscience, beseeching him that my
part be not in the blood of Christ if I wrote
of all I have written throughout this book
aught of an evil purpose . . . or to stir up
any false doctrine or opinion in the Church
of Christ, or to be the author of any sect,
or to draw disciples after me."[2] Either this
man was an arrant hypocrite who proved

Tindale's time, examined three hundred and eleven clergymen in their theological attainments. Of this number he
reported that one hundred and seventy-one were unable to
repeat the Ten Commandments, ten could not say the Lord's
Prayer, twenty-seven could not tell who was its author, and
thirty did not know where it was to be found. See *English
Historical Review*, January, 1904, p. 98.

[1] *Preface to the Pentateuch.* The quotation is condensed.
[2] *Preface to New Testament*, 1534.

loyal to his hypocrisy through years of exile, neglect, and reproach and at last laid down his life in defence of his hidden shame, or these words are a faithful picture of a sincere and noble spirit. Common sense and an average knowledge of men may be safely left to make choice of these alternatives.

Let us now inquire as to Tindale's qualifications for the work. It is no exaggeration to say that the translation of the Bible is the most arduous literary task that any man can face. Certain intellectual qualities of the highest type are needed for the work. Accurate and wide linguistic scholarship; a first-hand knowledge of Greek and Hebrew abreast of the best learning of the time; a literary intuition that fixes instinctively on the word which fits exactly the thought to be conveyed; a genius for cadence, for rhythm, for the subtile and fugitive meanings of words—these are indispensable prerequisites. Moreover, spiritual qualifications are no less necessary. "The style is the man," is a saying true here as in the case of original literary effort. He who would catch the spirit of Holy Writ must himself be possessed with a love of the truth, with a passion for simplicity and reality. How stands Tindale when confronted with these high tests? Everywhere in his writings the transparent honesty of the man leaps out between the lines. The deeper religious spirit generated by the Reformation finds in him a signal embodiment. It was this new spirit working on a simple and conscientious nature that enabled Tindale to carry to success his great life-purpose. Even Sir Thomas More, his great literary opponent, bears testimony to the reputation Tindale had gained at the University. " He was well known," he says, " for a man of right good living, studious and well learned in Scripture." Unwavering loyalty to what he conceived to be the truth, earnest piety, clearness of mind, an Apostolic simplicity of life, are the qualities which shine out in his life as history knows him. It is in this seriousness, this veracity of soul, stamped on his work that we are to find in large measure the secret of its abnormal vitality.

On the literary side, we are struck by his mastery of the English language, his new feeling for English style. His original writings, though without the intellectual largeness which characterises the work of More, are yet superior to it as pieces of English literature. Tindale avoids the elaborate Latinism of More's style and has a greater sense of rhythm, a greater aptitude for brief, sententious, epigrammatic speech. This quality in no small degree fitted him for the translation of such a simple and loosely constructed language as the Hellenistic Greek of the New Testament. As has been said, " To him we may safely ascribe all the most important qualities of the translation, the energy, the contagious earnestness, the unassuming dignity, and the vividness by which it holds its place in our literature. He once for all in his version determined the style of the English Bible." [1]   His knowledge of

[1] J. H. Gardiner, *The Bible as English Literature*, p. 327.

New Testament Greek and his independence as a translator have now been established beyond all doubt by such investigators as Westcott, Mombert, Moulton, Eadie, and others. Of his Hebrew scholarship, something will be said in a moment. Meantime, that we may the better understand the greatness of his task, a glance at his helps and hindrances is necessary.

For the Greek he had the printed Greek of the New Testament, which, up till its publication by Erasmus, was accessible only in manuscripts. The second and third editions appeared in 1519 and 1522. Tindale studied the three editions, but was especially guided by the last. Then he was much influenced by Luther's German version of the New Testament, published in 1522, and some of the happiest renderings in our English New Testament we owe indirectly to the German reformer. His third help was the Latin translation which accompanied the Greek text of Erasmus. It was this Latin rendering which held the first place, next to the

Greek, in the estimate of Tindale. Finally, he had recourse to the Latin Vulgate. For the Old Testament he had the Hebrew Bible, five editions of which had been printed between 1488 and 1525, Luther's translation, and the Vulgate. For the whole Bible he was able to consult Wycliffe's translation, the influence of which, however, is much less in the Old than in the New Testament. It would be a mistake, however, to suppose that he depended on Wycliffe's version as the groundwork of his translation. That he was familiar with the manuscripts of Wycliffe's work can not be questioned. Again and again he takes over a phrase from the fourteenth century translator.[1] As to his originality and independence, his own express statement must receive full weight. '' I had,'' he says, '' no man to counterfeit, neither was helped with English of any that had interpreted the same or such like thing in the Scripture aforetime.''[2]

[1] See Appendix, Note B.

[2] *Epistle to the Reader*, New Testament, 1525. Any one can verify for himself the truth of Tindale's claim by a reference

On the other side must be counted his hindrances. To begin with, the only text accessible to him was poor and faulty in the extreme. The manuscripts from which Erasmus constructed his New Testament were not merely few and late but—and this was their real weakness—belonged to the "Syrian group," to use Westcott and Hort's nomenclature, which originated by a process of revision in the fourth century, and is therefore not the best representative text. Hence many of his mistakes were due to the faulty Greek which he had to work with.

In the second place, there was not then as now an embarrassment of riches in the way of the mechanical helps, such as commentaries, concordances, lexicons, etc. As a consequence, unintentional mistakes could not but happen. Then again, the science of textual criticism was not yet born. Nobody discussed variant readings or balanced nicely the authority for this or that phrase. In-

to the passages from Wycliffe's translation given in the Appendix.

accuracy in details was found to characterise
a translation effected on such an unscientific
basis. Finally, we must not carry back into
the sixteenth century the modern ideal of a
translator. Tindale too often neglects the
connecting Greek particles, is occasionally
misled by the Vulgate, sometimes paraphrases rather than translates, and once and
again falls into positive blunders.[1]

The true monument to Tindale's genius is
to be found in the fact that nearly four hundred years have passed away since he died,
and yet our latest version retains not only
the greater portion by far of his diction, but
the very structural mould in which his translation was set. Language is a living thing,
and life means movement, change, progress.
Yet just as a tree or plant preserves con-
tinuity of form beneath all vital processes
and is ever true to itself, so the English Bible
retains the shape, the outline, first sketched
by the master hand. To take an illustration,

---

[1] See Eadie, *The English Bible*, Vol. I, pp. 151-154, for
some of these blunders.

the Epistle to the Galatians is a piece of
Greek which taxes a translator's powers to
the utmost; yet the fact remains that about
five-eighths of the whole are retained in the
Revision from Tindale's translation. It is to
him we owe in a large measure those winged
words and verbal felicities that have passed
into the life-blood of our higher speech, that
diction at once majestic and tender, elevated
and simple, which has won the admiration of
a Faber and a Carlyle, of a Newman and a
Matthew Arnold, and which has become the
current coin of religious speech. Space will
permit but a few examples of what lies on
every page of the New Testament. " Ye
cannot serve God and mammon." [1] " Consider the lilies of the field, how they grow." [2]
" Wide is the gate, and broad is the way, that
leadeth to destruction " [3] (suggested by
Wycliffe). " Where two or three are gathered together in my name, there am I in the
midst of them." [4] " He came to himself." [5]
" I have sinned against heaven, and in thy

[1] Matt. vi. 24.   [3] Matt. vii. 13.   [5] Luke xv. 17.
[2] Matt. vi. 28.   [4] Matt. xviii. 20.

sight." [1] " A prophet hath no honour in his
own country." [2] " In my Father's house
are many mansions " [3] (suggested by the
Vulgate). " A chosen vessel." [4] " In him
we live, and move, and have our being." [5]
" It is more blessed to give than to receive." [6]
" Let us do evil, that good may come." [7]
" There is no fear of God before their
eyes." [8] " The Spirit of adoption, whereby
we cry, Abba, Father." [9] " When I was a
child, I spake as a child." [10] " The un-
searchable riches of Christ." [11] " The love
of Christ which [love] passeth knowledge." [12]
" Turned to flight the armies of the
aliens." [13] " The tongue can no man
tame." [14] " Out of darkness into his marvellous light." [15] " Who did no sin, neither
was guile found in his mouth." [16] " The
Shepherd and Bishop of your souls." [17]

Not the least impressive element in the

[1] Luke xv. 21.
[2] John iv. 44.
[3] John xiv. 2.
[4] Acts ix. 15.
[5] Acts xvii. 28.
[6] Acts xx. 35.
[7] Rom. iii. 8.
[8] Rom. iii. 18.
[9] Rom. viii. 15.
[10] I. Cor. xiii. 11.
[11] Eph. iii. 8.
[12] Eph. iii. 19.
[13] Heb. xi. 34.
[14] James iii. 8.
[15] I. Pet. ii. 9.
[16] I. Pet. ii. 22
[17] I. Pet. ii. 25.

Revisers' debt to Tindale is the number of places where they have gone back to renderings of his that had been excluded from the Authorised Version. A striking illustration is found in St. Paul's glorious hymn to Love,[1] which for the Apostle was no abstract virtue, but had taken to itself hands and feet in the person of the Incarnate Son of God. Our Revisers displace the narrow and now misleading word " charity " by " love "— the expression which alone had seemed adequate to Tindale. Other examples may be seen in single words or brief phrases that yet affect the sense materially. Thus, the expressions italicised in the following are restored from his text: " Ye *shall therefore* [R.V. *therefore shall*] be perfect."[2]   " He *that was sown.*"[3]   " When the wine *failed.*"[4] " Except a man be born *anew.*"[5]   " One *flock,* one shepherd."[6]   " *Believe in God,*"[7] instead of, " Ye believe in God."   " *In the sight of* God."[8]   " *In* the name of Jesus."[9]

[1] Cor. xiii.
[2] Matt. v. 48.
[3] Matt. xiii. 19, 20, 22.
[4] John ii. 3.
[5] John iii. 3.
[6] John x. 16.
[7] John xiv. 1.
[8] II Cor. xii. 19.
[9] Phil. ii. 10.

" If *he* withdraw himself."[1]   " Shutteth
up *his compassion* from him."[2]

In some passages, the Revisers have restored, not indeed Tindale's actual words,
but the substance of his renderings.[3] A good
example is found in Jude, verse 12, where
Tindale had rendered " trees without fruit
at gathering time "—a rendering for which
the Authorised Version substituted, wrongly,
" trees whose fruit withereth, without fruit."
The Revisers substantially restore Tindale's
translation—" autumn trees without fruit."

Let us now return to Tindale's work in the
Old Testament. It has been almost a tradition among writers who have not made any
personal investigation of the matter to suppose that while Tindale may have been a
competent Greek scholar, his qualifications
for translating the Old Testament were very

[1] Heb. x. 37.   [2] John iii. 17.

[3] For other illustrations compare Mark iv. 13, vi. 14, xi. 17 ;
John xii. 13, xv. 20 ; Acts ii. 23, xx. 10, xxiii. 27 ; Romans
i. 18 ; I Thes. iv. 14 ; II Thes. i. 10, ii. 8 ; Heb. xi. 13.   Compare also II Cor. iii. 5, 6, where the connection in the Greek
is brought out by Tindale in a way similar to that followed by
the Revisers.

meagre. This idea has been recently repeated by a distinguished Roman Catholic
scholar.[1]   Now it might be sufficient to reply
on general grounds that if Tindale is, as even
his critics acknowledge, the real Father of
the English Bible, and if the substance of his
translation in the Old Testament is retained
in our latest Revision, on which the ablest
Hebraists of our times were engaged, it follows that he cannot have been so innocent
of Hebrew as some suppose.   We may admit
that there was but small opportunity for him
to acquire the language during his stay in
England; but his long sojourn in Germany,
his known contact with the circle of the German reformers, some of whom were enthu-
siasts in Old Testament studies, gave him
abundant opportunity to get a good working
knowledge of the subject.   Moreover, literary

[1] Rev. Prof. Francis E. Gigot, in his otherwise scholarly
book, *General Introduction to the Study of the Scriptures*, p.
359, says : " William Tyndale, a Franciscan priest, who, having turned out a Protestant, undertook to publish a translation
of the whole Bible from the original text, though he had
but little knowledge of Hebrew." There are several inac-
curacies in this statement.

helps in his undertaking were not wanting.
In 1506, Reuchlin, who introduced the study
of Hebrew into Germany, published his
Rudiments of the Hebrew Language, and
this was followed by other grammatical and
lexical works by the disciples of Reuchlin—
Sebastian Münster, Sanctes Pagninus, Matthew Aurigallus, and others. Moreover,
five Hebrew Bibles had been printed between
1488 and 1530, and the famous Complutentian
Polyglott which contained the Septuagint,
appeared in 1514. So far, then, we can say
that he had both opportunity and help available for the work of Old Testament translation. Then we have an implied claim to the
knowledge of Hebrew scattered throughout
his various writings. In his answer to More,
he speaks of the Hebrew text as " of most
need to be known," implying his acquaintance with it. In his Epistle to the Reader
prefixed to his *Revised New Testament* of
1534, he discourses on the genius of the
Hebrew language in a way possible only to
one who had made a study of it. He knows,

for example, that "in Hebrew the preter-
perfect tense and present tense is often both
one, and the future tense is the optative
mood, and the future tense often the impera-
tive mood in the active voice, and in the pas-
sive ever, and likewise person for person,
number for number, and an interrogation for
a conditional, and such like is with the
Hebrews a common usage." There is still
extant an original letter, addressed by Tindale in the winter of 1535, while a prisoner
at Vilvorde, to the Governor of Vilvorde
Castle, in which he makes the following
pathetic petition: "But above all I entreat
and beseech your clemency to be urgent with
the Procureur that he may kindly permit me
to have my Hebrew Bible, Hebrew grammar,
and Hebrew dictionary, that I may spend my
time with that study." [1]

But actual proof of Tindale's Hebrew
scholarship has now been made. It has been
shown recently by a comparison of his text

[1] For a facsimile of this letter, see Demaus, *William Tindale*, p. 536.

with the Vulgate, the Septuagint, the
Hebrew, and with Wycliffe's and Luther's
translations, that though he did not make a
literal unaided version from the Hebrew, as
if no other translation existed, he yet used
his helps with scholarly independence, and
in some places goes against the preceding
versions, relying solely on his own judgment.[1]
The conclusion arrived at is " that Tindale,
in translating his Pentateuch, kept constantly
before him the Hebrew text and Luther's
version, with the Septuagint and Vulgate
within easy reach, and fragments of the
Middle English archaisms running through
his mind as he worked; that he probably made
his first draft from the German, checking it
constantly by the Hebrew and departing
from it in nearly every case where he detected
Luther in an evasion; that he carried into
this work the same principle already established in his New Testament, of making an

[1] See J. R. Slater, *The Sources of Tindale's Version of the
Pentateuch, a Dissertation for the Degree of Doctor of Philoso-
phy*, Chicago, 1906.

idiomatic English work in the language of
the common people rather than of the
learned; transferring such Semitic idioms as
approved themselves to him as easily understood and more vigorous than paraphrase." [1]
Many of the Hebrew idioms which Tindale
took over have become the commonplaces of
religious speech and are retained in the
Revised Version. A few may here be cited:
" To die the death "; " the Lord's an-
ointed "; " the gate of heaven "; " thorn
in the side " ; " a man after his own heart ";
" the living God "; " sick unto death ";
" flowing with milk and honey "; " to fall
by the sword "; " the horn of my salvation "; " smote them hip and thigh"; " as
the Lord liveth "; " in the beauty of holiness " (R.V. margin); " the blast of thy
nostrils "; " uncircumcised lips "; " to seek
his face "; " sacrifices of righteousness ";
" strengthen the heart "; " plagued with
plagues "; " old and full of days "; " men
of renown "; "integrity of my heart "; " in-

[1] *Ibid.*, p. 54.

nocency of my hands "; " greatness of thine
excellency "; " greatness of thine arm."
" He felt, by a happy instinct," remarks
Westcott, " the potential affinity between
Hebrew and English idioms, and enriched our
language and thought forever with the char-
acteristics of the Semitic mind." [1]   Taking
almost at random two passages, Deuteronomy
vi. 4-9, and Numbers xvi. 31-35, we find that
Tindale translates the former passage with
one hundred and twelve words, of which the
Revised Version retains ninety-three, and
the latter passage with one hundred and sixteen words, of which ninety-three are also
retained.   The more his work is studied, the
more is its originality apparent, and it is this
originality that to a considerable extent has
created the antique and dignified cast of
sentences which lifts the Bible out of the
ruck of ordinary literature and makes it a
book apart.

[1] *History of the English Bible*, p. 158.

CHAPTER II

WHILE Tindale was awaiting execution in Vilvorde Castle, a change was passing over the authorities in England. Henry's external and ecclesiastical reformation included an authorised English translation of the Scriptures. Owing to Tindale's Lutheran sympathies, his work had from the first been discredited in the eyes of the King, who regarded Luther as a blasphemous heresiarch, and hated all his doings with a perfect hatred. But though he prohibited Tindale's translation, he promised at the same time a properly accredited version. This was in 1530. In 1534 the King was reminded of his promise by a petition from Convocation, as he had been reminded in 1530 by a letter ascribed, but without any historical warrant, to Hugh Latimer.

27

His astute political agent, Cromwell, read aright the signs of the times, took a quiet scholar named Miles Coverdale into his pay, and set him to the work of Biblical translation.[1] Mr. Gairdner holds that the Bishops in 1534 set about translating the New Testament. We know as a matter of fact that Bishop Gardiner translated St. Luke and St. John. It would appear that Cromwell had taken an old translation of the New Testament, divided it into nine or ten parts, and sent them to the " best learned bishops," to be corrected.[2] It is possible that this lost translation may turn up some day.[3]

We could wish for more knowledge of Coverdale's personality than history affords, for he stands second only to Tindale in the line of men who have consecrated their lives and talents to the work of translating the Bible. Only within recent years has justice

[1] *Remains of Coverdale*, p. 490.

[2] Strype, *Cranmer*, I, 48-49.

[3] See Gairdner, *Lollardy and the Reformation in England*, Vol. II, p. 268.

been done to his fine delicacy, the tender beauty of his phrases, the musical charm of his renderings. A recent writer pays a just tribute to his literary aptitudes. " It is," he says, " to the melodiousness of his phrasing, to his mastery over what may be described as the literary semi-tone, to his innumerable dexterities and felicitous turns of expression, that we owe more probably than we most of us recognise of that strangely moving influence which seems ever to be welling up from the perennial springs of the English Bible." [1] We owe Coverdale another debt of gratitude. Words sanctioned by long ecclesiastical usage, such as " confess," " church," " grace," " contrite," which had been challenged by Tindale, owing to the popular misuse of them, were restored to the text by Coverdale, whose irenical spirit loved to mingle the old with the new. He saw these words laden, as it were, with the emotion, the thought, the sacred associations, of centuries, and he could not let them go.

[1] Hoare, *The Evolution of the English Bible,* p. 178.

Coverdale was born in 1488, studied at Cambridge, was ordained to the priesthood in 1514, and a little later became an Augustinian friar. In some way or other, he attracted the notice of Cromwell. An undated letter of his, written to the great minister, is still extant, in which he speaks with enthusiasm of his Biblical studies. About 1523, he went over to the side of the Reformation and the new learning. Some time later he threw aside the friar's habit and assumed that of a secular priest. Seeking safety on the Continent, there is reason to believe that he met Tindale at Hamburg in 1529, and that for the next five years or so he was engaged in the translation of the Bible, which appeared in 1535. The University of Tübingen made him a Doctor of Divinity, and in 1551 he was consecrated Bishop of Exeter, only, however, to be deprived of his see on the accession of Mary. On Elizabeth's accession he returned to England, but owing to his objections to vestments and legal church ceremonies he could not resume his bishopric.

Later he became Vicar of St. Magnus Church, London, dying there in 1568.

His Bible was put through the press abroad, and appeared in England in 1536, with a dedication to the King. This was the first complete printed English Bible. It differs from Tindale's in being only a secondary version " made out of five sundry interpreters," these being, as is now generally agreed, the Swiss-German, or Zürich version (1524-1529), the Latin version of Sanctes Pagninus (1528), the Vulgate, Luther's German Bible, and Tindale's translation. With singular modesty and ability, he sets forth the reasons for his undertaking the work of translation. " Considering," he says, " how excellent knowledge and learning an interpreter of scripture ought to have in the tongues, and pondering also mine own insufficiency therein, and how weak I am to perform the office of a translator, I was the more loath to meddle with this work. Notwithstanding, when I considered how great pity it was that we should want it so long and called to my

remembrance the adversity of them which
were not only of ripe knowledge, but would
also with all their hearts have performed that
they began if they had not had impediment; [1]
considering, I say, that by reason of their adversity, it could not so soon have been
brought to an end as our most prosperous na-
tion would fain have had it, these and other
reasonable causes considered, I was the more
bold to take it in hand." Does any one ob-
ject that the multiplication of translations of
the Bible leads to schisms and to confusion?
Coverdale replies: " That is not so; for it
was never better with the congregation of
God than when every church almost had the
Bible of a sundry translation. Among the
Greeks, had not Origen a special translation?
Had not Vulgarius one peculiar, and likewise
Chrysostom? Besides the seventy interpreters, is there not the translation of Aquila,
of Theodotion, of Symmachus, and of sundry
other? Again among the Latin men, thou

---

[1] The allusion is to Tindale, who at this time was a
prisoner.

findest that every one almost used a special and sundry translation." He defends the translation of the same Greek and Hebrew words by different English expressions on the ground that there is no real diversity between these different renderings. Hence he translates the same Greek word in one place by the word " penance " and in another place by the word " repentance." [1]

It is to Coverdale's literary instinct that the Revised Version is indebted for some of those renderings whose appealing power can never be lost; as for example: " There will the eagles be gathered together " [Tindale: " Even thither will the eagles resort "]; [2] " Enter thou into the joy of thy Lord " [Tindale: " Enter in into thy Master's joy "]; [3] " crucified unto me, and I unto the world " [Tindale: " Crucified as touching me and I as concerning the world "]; [4] " None of us liveth to himself, and none dieth to himself " [Tindale: " For none of us liveth his own

---

[1] See *Prologue* to Coverdale's Bible.   [3] Matt. xxv. 21.
[2] Matt. xxiv. 28.   [4] Gal. vi. 14.

servant: neither doth anyone of us die his
own servant ''];[1] '' Death is swallowed up in
victory '' [Tindale: '' Death is consumed into
victory ''];[2] '' The world passeth away ''
[Tindale: '' The world vanisheth away ''].[3]

In 1538, Coverdale published a Latin-Eng-
lish New Testament in which the Vulgate and
an English translation were set side by side.
Of this book three editions appeared, one
only, however, with the approval of Coverdale. It has been discovered that the Rhemish translators consulted this New Testament (doubtless because of their reverence
for the Vulgate) and took over from it many
felicitous and harmonious turns of expression. The Revised Version has been
made heir to some of these. For example, in
Romans viii. 3, the Rhemists improve on
their predecessors by the rendering, '' *in that*
it was weakened through the flesh,'' but they
owe the improvement to Coverdale's Dig-
lott.[4]

[1] Rom. xiv. 7.   [2] I. Cor. xv. 54.   [3] I. John ii. 17.

[4] See Carleton, *Part of Rheims in the Making of the
English Bible*, pp. 7, 8.

At this point it is necessary to notice the appearance of another Bible. This is the real *editio princeps* of the English Bible. It arrived in England in 1537, bearing the name of Thomas Matthew, and the English title-page bore the words, " set forth with the King's most gracious license." It is a compilation consisting of Tindale's revised New Testament [1] and Pentateuch, in addition to which was his translation left in manuscript containing the books of Joshua to II Chronicles, inclusive. This manuscript material, as has been said, fell into the hands of John Rogers, the first to suffer death for the new opinions in the reign of Mary. The parts left untranslated by Tindale were taken from Coverdale's Bible. It is obvious that Matthew's text has no claim to originality, but its historical importance lies in the fact that it represents the basal text of our Revised Version. It was Matthew's text which at Cromwell's instigation Coverdale took as his basis for a new revision. This work, begun in

[1] 1535, 1534 edit.

Paris in 1538, but interrupted by the hostile action of the Inquisition, was transferred to England, and issued in April, 1539, as the first edition of a Bible which from its size came to be known as the " Great Bible." Seven editions of it were issued 1539-1541. Of this series, the fourth edition, by a curious irony, bore the name of Tunstall, Bishop of Durham, the prelate who refused to countenance Tindale or his work.

The helps which Coverdale used for his revision of the Old Testament were Sebastian Münster's Latin translation and his own translation as given in his Bible of 1535. In the New Testament he revises Tindale's text with the help of Erasmus's Latin translation and his own version of 1535.

The Great Bible presents some of the renderings of Coverdale's Bible in a finished form, and these have enriched our latest version. As illustrations take, for example: " His eyelids try the children of men ";[1] " Deliver my soul from the sword; my

[1] Ps. xi. 4.

darling from the power of the dog ";[1] " Yea,
though I walk through the valley of the
shadow of death, I will fear no evil : for thou
art with me; thy rod and thy staff they com-
fort me ";[2] " My tongue is the pen of a
ready writer ";[3] " [truth] in the inward
parts ";[4] " Cast me not away from thy
presence; and take not thy holy spirit from
me ";[5] " like a lodge in a garden of cucum-
bers ";[6] " the chastisement of our peace ";[7]
" The fathers have eaten sour grapes, and
the children's teeth are set on edge ";[8] " But
unto you that fear my name shall the Sun of
righteousness arise."[9]

Readers familiar with the Prayer Book
Psalter need no quotations to prove Coverdale's marvellous ear for sound and appre-
ciation of the poetic element in language.
This version is the permanent monument to
his genius. When we come to his treatment
of Tindale's work, we find touches which,

[1] Ps. xxii. 20.
[2] Ps. xxiii. 4.
[3] Ps. xlv. 1.
[4] Ps. li. 11
[5] Isa. i. 8.
[6] Ps. li. 6.
[7] Isa. liii. 5.
[8] Jer. xxxi. 29.
[9] Mal. iv. 2.

though apparently slight, are immense improvements on the original translator's work. As illustrations, take the following: "Till heaven and earth *pass* away ";[1] "but *considerest* not the beam that is in thine own eye ";[2] " But while men slept, *his enemy came* ";[3] " Friend, *how camest thou in hither* ";[4] " *Lord, Lord,* open to us ";[5] " Fathers, *provoke not* your children ";[6] " God *cannot be tempted with evil* ";[7] " the Father of *lights.*"[8]

The ecclesiastical reaction which marked the end of Henry's reign now set in, and no new translation was attempted for about twenty years. Various restrictions were placed upon popular Bible reading. No " artisan, labourer, apprentice, or servant " was permitted to enjoy the privilege on pain of imprisonment. The confusions of the royal mind were reflected in paradoxical enactments which forbade Tindale's and Cover-

[1] Matt. v. 18. [3] Matt. xiii. 25. [5] Matt. xxv. 11.
[2] Matt. vii. 3. [4] Matt. xxii. 12. [6] Col. iii. 21.
[7] James i. 13 (Great Bible May, Nov., 1540).
[8] James i. 17.

dale's versions, yet gave free course to the
Great Bible, in which these were substantially
preserved.[1]

[1] A translation of the Bible marked by individual
peculiarities appeared in 1539 bearing the name of Richard
Taverner, a lawyer of the Inner Temple. His work has had
no great influence on our received English text. It has
had, however, a very distinct influence on the Rhemish
Version. No doubt the common link between some of
Taverner's renderings and those of the Rhemists is the
Vulgate; still there can be no question that the Rhemists
had Taverner's work before them. In this way, some of his
idiomatic and vigorous renderings have come into our
English Bible. Taverner's edition was a revision of Matthew's text.

CHAPTER III

THE CONTRIBUTION OF THE GENEVAN VERSION

HENRY died in the midst of the Catholic reaction, and Edward VI. came to the throne in 1547. The pendulum now swung to the Reformed side. Shortly after his accession, all restraints on the use of the Bible were removed. An injunction was issued calling upon all clergymen to set up in some convenient place within the church '' one book of the whole Bible of the largest volume in English '' and within a year '' the paraphrase of Erasmus also in English upon the Gospels.'' [1] Thus the Great Bible was restored to place and honour.

On his death and the accession of Mary, the hopes of the anti-Reformation party revived. To her fanatical, if thoroughly con-

[1] Cardwell, *Doc. Ann.*, I, 2, p. 9.

scientious spirit, Henry's policy of religious
harmony with yet ecclesiastical independence
of the Roman See appeared utterly unintel-
ligible. The public use of the Bible was once
more proscribed, and its champions fled for
refuge to the Continent. Here a number
more radical than the rest took refuge in
Geneva, the great stronghold of the new
movement and the home of Beza and Calvin;
and here they produced a version which,
though not in the direct line of descent, has
left a great mark through succeeding versions on our latest text. The Genevan Version is in the main the work of three men,
William Whittingham, Anthony Gilby, and
Thomas Sampson. All three were university
scholars.

William Whittingham [1] had been Fellow of
All Souls, Oxford. He had also studied at
Orléans and Paris and had visited some of
the German universities. During his travels,
he had come into contact with the Calvinistic
Reformers and had thrown in his lot with

[1] *National Dict. of Biog.*

them. He succeeded John Knox as Minister
to the English Congregation in Geneva in
1559. Returning to England some time after
Elizabeth's accession, he was appointed
Chaplain to Dudley, Earl of Warwick, and
was present at the siege of Havre, where
" his religious zeal and other services of a
more warlike character won him general
praise." In spite of his extreme Protestant-
ism, he was made Dean of Durham in 1563.
While in Geneva, he published a version of
the New Testament (1557), which was based
on Tindale. It was a distinct advance in
form on any version that had preceded it.
It was the first English New Testament
printed in Roman type, and the first to adopt
the division into verses which was made by
Stephens in his Greek Testament of 1551.
Whittingham no doubt borrowed this device
from a French Bible revised by Calvin,
which appeared at Geneva in 1556 and which
is the first translation of the entire Bible into
a modern language in which the chapters are
divided into verses and in which each verse

has prefixed to it its number in Arabic figures.[1]

Anthony Gilby[2] was a graduate of Cambridge University and was noted as a great controversialist on the Reformed side. On his return from Geneva, whither he had gone into exile on the accession of Mary, he was appointed to the living of Ashby in Leicestershire, where it is said that " he was respected for his godly life and learning " until his death in 1585. Gilby came into conflict once and again with the ecclesiastical authorities because of his opposition to the legal ceremonies of the Church. He showed his scholarship in various theological treatises and in original commentaries on Micah and Malachi.

Thomas Sampson[2] was also a Cambridge man, who studied law for a time in London. He became a Protestant and an enthusiastic Calvinist. On his return from his Genevan

---

[1] A French New Testament containing the same verse division was published in Geneva in 1553.

[2] *National Dict. of Biog.*

exile, he was made Canon of Durham in 1560 and Dean of Christ Church in 1561. Most of his life was spent in acrimonious theological controversy, and for a time he felt the restraining hand of Elizabeth, who issued a special order for his imprisonment.

These scholars, with the help of Coverdale and Knox, issued the complete Bible in 1560, henceforth to be known as the " Genevan Version." It was heralded by a separate edition of the Book of Psalms, published in 1559 and dedicated to Queen Elizabeth " as a special token of their service and good-will till the rest of the Bible, which was in good readiness, should be accomplished and presented." The basis of the Genevan Version in the Old Testament was the Great Bible, which was carefully compared with the Hebrew, and in the New Testament, Whittingham's version (which was itself a revision of Tindale's last revision), revised by the help of Beza's Latin version and of the Huguenot Bible edited by Calvin. The time occupied in the work of revision was " two years and

more, day and night.'' [1] '' It was,'' says
Edgar, '' the sweet fruit of suffering, and
it contained notes unmistakably evangelical,
sublimely predestinarian, conspicuously anti-
papal, and slyly democratic.'' [2] Unquestionably, of all the versions between Tindale's
and the Authorised, this is the most interesting and most worthy of study. It marked
a distinct advance in external form on its
predecessors. Issued in a handy quarto instead of a heavy folio, it was more suitable
for popular use. It followed Whittingham's
New Testament, moreover, in being printed
in Roman instead of black letters and in having the chapters divided into verses, with a
different type for those words which had
nothing corresponding to them in the original. Its popularity was unbounded. The
English middle classes and Scotchmen of all
ranks saw in it a great manifesto of the
Reformation. Westcott remarks that though
from the time of its first appearance '' it be-

[1] See *Preface* to *Genevan Bible*.
[2] *Bibles of England*, p. 151.

came the household Bible of the English-speaking nations,'' it was never sanctioned for public use in churches.[1] This is not quite accurate, for, though not authorised in England, it became the version sanctioned in Scotland both by Church and State.   The Scottish General Assembly ordered every parish to buy a copy for public use,[2] and it has been shown that Anglican preachers used it quite freely even after the Authorised Version had made its appearance.[3]   One other point of interest in connection with its history is that it was the version used by Shakespeare.[4]   It was printed again and again, till toward the end of the eighteenth century, and one hundred and sixty editions of it have been identified.

[1] *History of the English Bible*, 3d edit., p. 93.

[2] Comp. Darlow and Moule's *Historical Catalogue*, Vol. I, p. 89, under *Geneva Version* :   '' An Act of the Scots Parliament passed in 1579 ordered every householder worth 300 merks of yearly rent, and every yeoman or burgess worth £500 stock, to have a Bible and Psalm Book, in the vulgar language, in his house, under the penalty of ten pounds.''

[3] See *Authorisation of English Bible*, Macmillan's Magazine, October, 1881.

[4] See Carter, *Shakespeare and Holy Scripture*, pp. 1–19.

The translation itself is marked by scholarship, literary tact, and, when we consider the position of the authors, singular freedom from dogmatic prepossession. Modern opinion accepts the judgment of the translators on their own work when they say, " We may with good conscience protest that we have in every point and word, according to the measure of that knowledge which it pleased Almighty God to give us, faithfully rendered the text, and in all hard places most sincerely expounded the same. For God is our witness that we have by all means endeavoured to set forth the purity of the Word and the right sense of the Holy Ghost for the edifying of the brethren in faith and charity." [1]

The main weakness of the version was its too great reliance on Beza's text and the dogmatic colouring of its notes. Nevertheless, it inherited the fruits of Beza's insight into the meaning of the text, and this heritage has to a great degree been embodied in our latest revision. Not infrequently the Genevan

[1] *Preface* to the *Genevan Bible*, 1560.

Bible introduced correct renderings, which, rejected by the Authorised Version, have been taken back by our Revisers, though in some instances in different phraseology. Among these the following may be noted: " Use no vain repetitions." [1] " Cast out the mote." [2] " A house divided against a house falleth." [3] " Salvation is of the Jews." [4] " Because the Fast was now past." [5] " Abstain from all kind of evil." [6] " Shadowing by turning." [7] " And if ye call him Father." [8] One touch of modernity is especially striking—the name of St. Paul is omitted from the title of the Epistle to the Hebrews.

Many phrases and verses that have become the current coin of Christian speech and are stamped with the seal of the Revisers came first from the mint of the Genevan translators; e.g., " Canst thou by searching find out God? Canst thou find out the Almighty to

[1] Matt. vi. 7.   [4] John iv. 22.   [7] James i. 17.
[2] Matt. vii. 4.   [5] Acts xxvii. 9.   [8] I Peter i. 17.
[3] Luke xi. 17.   [6] I Thes. v. 22.

his perfection?"[1] "The house appointed for all living."[2] "Vanity of vanities, saith the Preacher; vanity of vanities, all is vanity."[3] "Remember now [R.V. " also "] thy Creator in the days of thy youth."[4] "He shall see of the travail of his soul."[5] "The angel of his presence."[6] "The fountain of living waters."[7] "Is there no balm at [R.V. " in "] Gilead?"[8] "His compassions fail not."[9] "My people are destroyed for lack of knowledge."[10] "For they have sown [R.V. " sow "] the wind, and they shall reap the whirlwind."[11] "For who hath despised the day of small things?"[12] "And I will spare them, as a man spareth his own son that serveth him."[13] "Solomon in all his glory."[14] "My beloved Son in whom I am well pleased."[15] "It is good for us to be here."[16] "In the gall of bitterness and

[1] Job xi. 7.
[2] Job xxx. 23.
[3] Ecc. i. 2.
[4] Ecc. xii. 1.
[5] Isa. liii. 11.
[6] Isa. lxiii. 9.
[7] Jer. ii. 13.
[8] Jer. viii. 22.
[9] Lam. iii. 22.
[10] Hosea iv. 6.
[11] Hosea viii. 7.
[12] Zech. iv. 10.
[13] Mal. iii. 17.
[14] Matt. vi. 29.
[15] Matt. xvii. 5.
[16] Luke ix. 33.

[R.V. adds '' in ''] the bond of iniquity.'' [1]
'' Men of like passions with you.'' [2] '' Called
to be saints.'' [3] '' The oracles of God.'' [4]
'' We are more than conquerors.'' [5] '' A
disobedient and gainsaying people.'' [6] '' We
know in part, and we prophesy in part.'' [7]
'' Knowing therefore the terror [R.V.
'' fear ''] of the Lord, we persuade men.'' [8]
'' We walk by faith, not by sight.'' [9] '' The
word of reconciliation.'' [10] '' Let us not be
weary of [R.V. '' in ''] well-doing: for in due
season we shall reap, if we faint not.'' [11]
'' That he might fill all things.'' [12] '' His
eyes [R.V. '' the eyes of him ''] with whom
we have to do.'' [13]

All this gives an inadequate conception of
the debt of our modern version to the Genevan exiles. On every page of the Bible there
are touches from their hands which marked an
improvement on all preceding translations

[1] Acts viii. 23.
[2] Acts xiv. 15.
[3] Rom. i. 7.
[4] Rom. iii. 2.
[5] Rom. viii. 37.
[6] Rom. x. 21.
[7] I Cor. xiii. 9.
[8] II Cor. v. 11.
[9] II Cor. v. 7.
[10] II Cor. v. 19.
[11] Gal. vi. 9.
[12] Eph. iv. 10.
[13] Heb. iv. 13.

and which have commended themselves to modern scholars. A few may be given: " A root *out of* a dry ground."[1] " He was despised, and *rejected of men.*"[2] " We *esteemed* him not."[3] " *Surely* he hath borne our griefs, and *carried our sorrows.*"[4] " But if the salt have lost its *savour.*"[5] " Lay not up *for yourselves* treasures upon the earth."[6] " *Where he had been brought up.*"[7] " *Recovering of* sight to the blind."[8] " His *word was with authority.*"[9] " All the *living* that she had."[10] " His only *begotten* Son."[11] " It was the *preparation of the passover.*"[12] " Woven *from the top throughout.*"[13] " The Spirit himself *beareth witness with our spirit.*"[14] " *The redemption* of our body."[15] " The *image* of his Son."[16] " *A living* sacrifice."[17] " *Abhor* that which is evil."[18] " Unto Jews a *stum-*

[1] Isa. liii. 2.
[2] Isa. liii. 3.
[3] Isa. liii. 3.
[4] Isa. liii. 4.
[5] Matt. v. 13.
[6] Matt. vi. 19.
[7] Luke iv. 16.
[8] Luke iv. 18.
[9] Luke iv. 32.
[10] Luke xxi. 4.
[11] John iii. 16.
[12] John xix. 14.
[13] John xix. 23.
[14] Rom. viii. 16.
[15] Rom. viii. 23.
[16] Rom. viii. 29.
[17] Rom. xii. 1.
[18] Rom. xii. 9.

bling-block." [1] *" Comparing spiritual things with spiritual* [things]." [2] " We *have* the mind of Christ." [3] " As a wise *master-builder."* [4] " A little leaven *leaveneth the whole lump."* [5] " The cup of blessing which we bless, is it not a *communion* of the blood of Christ?" [6] " A great door and *effectual."* [7] *" Able ministers of* the new testament." [8] " Our *light affliction, which is for* the *moment."* [9] *" Ministry of reconciliation."* [10] " That we might become the *righteousness of God in him."* [11] *" Be not unequally yoked* with unbelievers." [12] *" Casting down imaginations."* [13] " A different gospel; *which is not another gospel."* [14] " The fulness of the time." [15] " Weak and beggarly *rudiments."* [16] " As many as desire *to make a fair show in the flesh."* [17] *" Dispensation of the fulness of the time."* [18] *" What is the*

[1] I Cor. i. 23.
[2] I Cor. ii. 13.
[3] I Cor. ii. 16.
[4] I Cor. iii. 10.
[5] I Cor. v. 6.
[6] I Cor. x. 16.

[7] I Cor. xvi. 9.
[8] II Cor. iii. 6.
[9] II Cor. iv. 17.
[10] II Cor. v. 18.
[11] II Cor. v. 21.
[12] II Cor. vi. 14.

[13] II Cor. x. 5.
[14] Gal. i. 6-7.
[15] Gal. iv. 4.
[16] Gal. iv. 9.
[17] Gal. vi. 12.
[18] Eph. i. 10.

hope of his calling? " [1] " *All the fulness of God.*" [2] " Being *darkened* in their understanding." [3] " The *recompense of* reward." [4] " *Cloud* of witnesses." [5] " Run with patience the *race.*" [6] *

[1] Eph. i. 18.   [3] Eph. iv. 18.   [5] Heb. xii. 1.
[2] Eph. iii. 19.   [4] Heb. xi. 26.   [6] Heb. xii. 1.

* The words italicised we owe to the Genevan.

CHAPTER IV

THE CONTRIBUTION OF THE BISHOPS' BIBLE

WITH the dawning of " the spacious times of great Elizabeth," the fortunes of the English Bible once more took a turn for the better. The new Queen indeed was no ardent advocate of the Scriptures. Secularised in temper, compromising in policy, her attitude, as Green remarks, towards the enthusiasm of her time was that of Lorenzo de Medici towards Savonarola. She refused " to able or disable " any of the current versions. Still, she reissued the injunction of Edward VI ordering a copy of the Great Bible to be set up in each church for public use, and encouraged all men to read it with great humility and reverence as the very lively Word of God.[1] The reign of this version lasted for about thirty years. Meantime the Genevan became the favourite for private study and reading.

[1] Cardwell, *Doc. Ann.*, I, 2, p. 9.

Clearly Archbishop Parker, with his feeling for uniformity and discipline, was open to the suggestion of a new revision, which it would appear came first from Richard Cox, Bishop of Ely, who had not forgotten his troubles with the makers of the Genevan Version at Frankfort. The Archbishop resolved on a revision of the authorised Great Bible. He divided up the work into sections, and these were distributed among, as Strype says, " able bishops and other learned men " to read and revise, each his allotted portion, adding marginal notes for the correction of the text. The first edition appeared in 1568. Giles Lawrence, Professor of Greek at Oxford and one of the best Greek scholars of his time, drew up a paper containing " notes of errors in the translation of the New Testament." He selects for criticism twenty-nine passages. Fifteen are not aptly translated; in eight, words and pieces of sentences are omitted; in two, superfluous words are inserted; two are mistranslated, giving rise to an error in doctrine; and in two, the moods and tenses of verbs are changed.[1] As a result, an amended edition was published four years later. The motive for the undertaking, as given in the Preface drawn up by Parker, is the neglect and scarcity of copies of the Great Bible. " And for that the copies thereof be so wasted that very many churches do want their convenient Bibles, it was thought good to some well disposed men to recognise [revise] the same Bible again into this form as it has now come out, with some further diligence in the printing, and with some more light added, partly in the translation, and partly in the order of the text, not as condemning the former translation which was followed mostly of any other translation, excepting the original text from which as little variance was made as was thought meet to such as took pains therein." [2] In a letter, however, addressed by Parker to Cecil, in which he asks that the Queen might license the revision, he gives as well an explanation

[1] Strypes, *Life of Parker*, Appendix 85.
[2] See *Preface* to the *Bishops' Bible*.

more to the point: "As for that in certain places be publicly used some translations which have not been laboured in your realm, having interspersed divers prejudicial notes, which might have been also well spared."[1] The allusion here is obviously to the Genevan Version.

Though in many ways a distinct advance on the Great Bible, the episcopal venture as a whole must be deemed a failure. For this several reasons may be suggested. The Elizabethan bishops, with some few exceptions such as Parker himself and Grindal, Bishop of London, were not men distinguished for learning.[2] There was not a Hebrew scholar of distinction among them, and their work in the Old Testament was therefore especially inadequate. In the second place, the aim of the translators was not set high enough. Their

[1] Quoted by Westcott, *History of the English Bible*, p. 100, foot note.

[2] It is curious that Bishop Jewell, of whom Richard Hooker said "that he was the worthiest divine Christendom bred these many years," was not asked to take part in the revision. In his earlier years, he had studied the versions of Tindale and Coverdale.

rules, which they interpreted with but little freedom, enjoined that they should " follow the common English translation [the Great Bible] used in the churches, and not to recede from it but where it varieth manifestly from the Hebrew or Greek original." The conservative temper of their minds and their peculiar ecclesiastical difficulties made any adequate work exceedingly difficult. In the mordant phrase of Charles Lamb, they appeared to have " encouraged one another in mediocrity." Finally, a collection of translations by different hands, fused into no organic whole and influenced too mechanically by the Great Bible, even to the copying of errors which had been corrected by the Genevan, had no promise of life and as a matter of fact was powerless to stem the popular demand for its Calvinistic rival. Although going forth with the sanction of Convocation, it never gained the popular suffrage, nor did it even gain an exclusive place in the churches. The Psalter of the Great Bible, a monument as we have seen to the genius of Miles Coverdale, had

grown so familiar to those accustomed to it
that the Bishops' new version of the Psalms
failed to dislodge it, and so in the second edition of 1572 we find the old and the new Psalter published side by side in parallel columns.

And yet it would be a mistake to suppose
that the Bishops' Bible has not left traces
of linguistic skill and singularly happy turns
of expression as a legacy to our latest text.
Thus we have the following:[1] " Blessed
are they that *have been persecuted* for righteousness' sake ";[2] " leave there thy *gift* ";[3]
" for it is *profitable* for thee that one of thy
members *should* perish ";[4] " *a writing* of
divorcement ";[5] " shalt perform *unto the
Lord thine oaths* ";[6] " if ye *salute* your
brethren only ";[7] " *faithless and perverse*
generation ";[8] " He will *miserably* destroy
those miserable men ";[9] " she of her *want*
did cast in all that she had ";[10] " *With de-*

[1] The words italicised are contributed by the Bishops'
Bible.

[2] Matt. v. 10.   [5] Matt. v. 31.   [8] Matt. xvii. 17.
[3] Matt. v. 24.   [6] Matt. v. 33.   [9] Matt. xxi. 41.
[4] Matt. v. 29.   [7] Matt. v. 47.

[10] Mark xii. 44.—Here is a touch rejected by the Author-

sire I have desired "; [1] " and they that have authority over them are called *Benefactors "*; [2] " but Jesus he delivered up to *their will "*; [3] " called *The place of a skull "*; [4] " the *work* of the law "; [5] " *as we are* [R.V. " be "] *slanderously reported "*; [6] " was able also *to perform "*; [7] " *joint heirs* with Christ "; [8] " a rock *of offence "*; [9] " your [spiritual] *service "*; [10] " overcome evil with *good "*; [11] " Love *worketh no ill to* his neighbour "; [12] " we shall all *stand* before the judgment-seat of Christ "; [13] " *Let not* [then] your good be evil spoken of "; [14] " that no flesh should *glory* before God "; [15] " my understanding *is unfruitful "*; [16] " for we are not ignorant of his *devices "*; [17] " For not he that

ised Version but approved by the Revisers. Westcott has reckoned that Eph. iv. 1-16 contains 17 new variations from the Great Bible. It is worth noting that of these only three verbatim and a fourth slightly altered have survived in the R.V.

[1] Luke xxii. 15.	[7] Rom. iv. 21.	[13] Rom. xiv. 10.
[2] Luke xxii. 25.	[8] Rom. viii. 17.	[14] Rom. xiv. 16.
[?] Luke xxiii. 25.	[9] Rom. ix. 33.	[15] I Cor. i. 29.
[4] John xix. 17.	[10] Rom. xii. 1.	[16] I Cor. xiv. 14.
[5] Rom. ii. 15.	[11] Rom. xii. 21.	[17] II Cor. ii. 11.
[6] Rom. iii. 8.	[12] Rom. xiii. 10.	

commendeth himself is approved, but whom the Lord *commendeth* "; [1] " *unspeakable* words, which it is not *lawful* for a man to utter "; [2] " children ought not to lay up for the *parents,* but the *parents* for the children "; [3] " he is a *debtor to do* the whole law "; [4] " what the riches of *the glory of his inherit-*ance "; [5] " *gave him to be* head "; [6] " *holiness of truth* "; [7] " *that he might present it* "; [8] " *I am in a strait betwixt the two, having the desire to depart* "; [9] " made *in the likeness of* men "; [10] " the *power* of his resurrection "; [11] " the word of the truth *of the* gospel "; [12] " unto all pleasing "; [13] " what is the riches of *the glory of this mystery* "; [14] " the rudiments of the world "; [15] " a *more excellent* sacrifice "; [16] " the *wrath* of the king "; [17] " time will *fail* me "; [18] " the fathers fell asleep." [19]

[1] II Cor. x. 18.   [3] II Cor. xii. 14.   [5] Eph. i. 18.
[2] II Cor. xii. 4.   [4] Gal. v. 3.   [6] Eph. i. 22.
[7] Eph. iv. 24—The Bishops' Version is the first to translate here correctly.
[8] Eph. v. 27.   [12] Col. i. 5.   [16] Heb. xi. 4.
[9] Phil. i. 23.   [13] Col. i. 10.   [17] Heb. xi. 27.
[10] Phil. ii. 27.   [14] Col. i. 27.   [18] Heb. xi. 32.
[11] Phil. iii. 10.   [15] Col. ii. 20.   [19] II Pet. iii. 4.

The main historical significance of the Bishops' text lies in the fact that its second edition was taken as the basis of the Authorised Version, and it is thus the lineal ancestor of our present Revision.

CHAPTER V

WE must now study another translation, which, of all the versions outside the direct line of descent, with the possible exception of the Genevan, has affected the Authorised and, through it, the Revised New Testament more powerfully than any other. This is the famous Roman Catholic version made at Rheims in 1582. Like the work of Tindale and the Genevan divines, it was the fruit of exile voluntarily suffered for conscience' sake. With the accession of Elizabeth in 1558, the efforts of her sister Mary to make England Roman Catholic were brought to naught. Penal enactments were passed against the old faith. Many divines and scholars fled to the Continent, and among them William Allen, Principal of St. Mary's Hall, Oxford, and Canon of York, afterwards made a Cardinal by Sixtus V, at the request of Philip II of Spain, in the hope that his well-known political ability would help in the reorganisation of the Church in England, should the Armada, as was expected, prove victorious.[1]

The one ambition of Allen's life was to restore England to the Roman communion, and the instruments on which he relied were missionary propaganda and political intrigue. He took in earnest the temporal penalties annexed to the papal excommunication of Elizabeth, and openly declared Philip to be the rightful heir to the English throne. He was deeply impressed with the great danger of a complete extinction of the old priesthood and of the consequent inability of the Roman Church to profit by any favourable turn affairs in England might take, and he communicated his fears to Dr. Vendeville, Professor of Canon Law in the University of Douay. The result was the founding of a college affiliated to this university in 1568 for the education of English youths who, unwilling to take the oath of supremacy,

[1] See *Douay Diaries*, p. lxxxiv.

could not matriculate at Oxford or Cambridge, and for the training of learned priests, who might take the place of the fast diminishing Marian clergy.[1] Later it became the centre of a great missionary propaganda, aiming at the reconversion of England to papal doctrine. Allen, who was made President of the college, was himself a theologian of eminence, the author of several controversial works, and one of the company of revisers chosen to edit a new edition of the Septuagint which was published by Sixtus V in 1587.[2]

Ten years passed away in earnest literary and scholastic activity. Then, owing to the hostility of the Huguenot townspeople, the college was compelled to remove to Rheims, where it received a friendly welcome. Here is the birthplace of the first Roman Catholic version of the New Testament in English. Among the subjects of collegiate study, the Bible held a prominent place. Every day a lecture was delivered on some passage of

[1] *Ibid.*, p. xxvii.   [2] *Ibid.*, p. lxxxiv.

Scripture. A chapter from the Old Testament and one from the New were expounded after dinner and supper daily, and during these meals Bible lessons were read. In this way, the Old Testament was gone over twelve times every three years or so, and the New Testament sixteen times in the same period. This information we owe to Allen himself,[1] who takes occasion at the same time to point out how seriously handicapped Roman Catholic preachers were, inasmuch as, being familiar only with the Vulgate, they often hesitated or blundered when trying, on the spur of the moment, to translate it into English. He proposes an English Catholic Version, and, if the Pope will permit, he undertakes to get the work done. A translation of the Scripture into barbarous tongues is not perhaps in itself desirable. Still, the curiosity of men not wholly bad and the need of a weapon wherewith to confute the heretics, as well as the peril to which the faithful

---

[1] *Ibid.*, p. xli. See also *Letters and Memorials of Cardinal Allen*, pp. 52 *seq.*

are exposed in reading existing versions, makes it at worst a necessary evil.[1] The source of this information is a letter, dated 1578.[2] Here, then, is the earliest germ of the enterprise.

We know when the work was begun and when it was finished. In the margin of the second Douay Diary, under date of October, 1578, we read: " On or about October 16th, Martin, graduate and Licentiate in Theology, began a version of the Bible in English in order to oppose most healthfully the corruptions of the heretics whereby they have sadly imposed for so long a time on almost all the people of our country, and that the work—a very useful one as is hoped—may issue the

[1] Robert Parsons, writing in 1580, says : " The Scripture is read there [in church] in false and shameless translations containing manifest and wilful corruptions to draw it to their own purposes, as hath been showed . . . and is like to be (shortly) more plainly by the grace of God."—*Reasons Why Catholics Refuse to Go to Church.*

[2] The letter from Allen to Vendeville is in Latin, and the original is preserved in the archives of the English College in Rome. It is printed in *Letters, etc., of Cardinal Allen,* pp. 52-67. The date is altered to 1580. If correct, Allen must have taken for granted the papal approbation.

more speedily, he finishes the translating of
two chapters daily. These chapters, for the
sake of greater correctness, Allen our President and Bristow our Moderator read over
carefully, and if anything anywhere seems
faulty, they in their wisdom faithfully correct
it.'' There is no record, strange to say, of
the progress of the work or of the mode of
procedure. One line records only its com-
pletion. Under date of March, 1582, we
read: '' In this month, the last touches were
given the New Testament edited in English.''

In 1593, the college returned to Douay,
where, sixteen years later, the Old Testament, translated by Martin and annotated
by Dr. Thomas Worthington, was published.
The long delay in its appearance is explained
in the Preface as due to '' our poor estate in
banishment.'' We owe the Douay Bible,
then, to a small group of distinguished Oxford scholars, who, in spite of their attach-
ment to the old faith, had unconsciously been
influenced by their contact with the new
learning. This group had for its central

figure Gregory Martin, with whom were associated as revisers William Allen, Richard
Bristow, Thomas Worthington, and William
Reynolds.[1] These men were eminently quali-
fied for their high labours. Martin was regarded by his contemporaries as a paragon of
learning. Admitted by the founder as one
of the original scholars of St. John's College,
Oxford, he had a brilliant academic career.
Anthony à Wood, the old Oxford chronicler,
speaks of him as " a most excellent linguist,
exactly read and versed in the Sacred Scriptures, and went beyond all of his time in
humane literature, whether in poetry or
prose." [2] His college had no one to match
him in Greek and Hebrew learning. If
Oxford gave him classical and philological
knowledge, Douay taught him theology. He
eventually became professor in the Seminary,
giving himself mainly to the work of trans-

[1] See Dodd, *Church History of England* (edit. 1739, Vol. II,
Part 4, Book 2). Possevino,—*Apparatus sacer* [under *Biblia ;*
margin *Anglica Editio*]. Whitaker, *Answere to a Certeine
Booke Written by Maister William Rainolds, etc.*, p. 365.

[2] *Athenæ Oxonienses*, Vol. I (under *Gregory Martin*).

lating the Bible and to writing a sharp criticism of the then existing English versions.
So eagerly did he pursue these tasks that
his health was undermined and he fell a
victim to tuberculosis. The year which saw
the issue of his New Testament was the year
of his death.

Bristow was the rhetorician of the party.
Full scope for his polemical gifts was found
in the uncompromising notes which, alas, for
controversial fame, lie neglected and forgotten in the original edition of the Rhemish
New Testament.[1] Most of the Douay divines
had come under the influence of the new
teaching at Oxford, and their belief in the
need and value of an English translation of
the Bible suited to serve their church in
England was no doubt unconsciously the
product of their early associations.

[1] Daniel O'Connell, the Irish liberator, himself a devout
Roman Catholic, denounced many of the Rhemish notes as
" odious and abominable " at a time when it was feared their
republication would prejudice the prospects of Catholic emancipation. See O'Connell's *Speeches*, edited by his son, Vol.
II, p. 257. The modern notes, while thoroughly ecclesiastical
in tone, are also perfectly inoffensive.

The version was made, not from the original Greek and Hebrew, but from the Latin Vulgate. The translators, however, had the original texts before them. " We translate," say the Rhemists, " the old vulgar Latin text, not the common Greek text," and they give reasons why they " translate the Latin text rather than the Hebrew." They offer ten reasons for their choice of a translation instead of the primary text as the basis of their work. Briefly put, they are as follows: The great antiquity of the Vulgate, its correction by St. Jerome with reference to the Greek text, its commendation by St. Augustine, its use in the public services of the church since that time, the confirmation of it as the authentic text of Scripture by the Council of Trent, its impartiality and freedom from bias, its great fidelity to the original, the preference shown for it by Protestants like Beza, its freedom from variations as compared with the endless diversity of reading in the common Greek text, its superiority to the Greek where it differs from it, " for most of the ancient heretics were Grecians and therefore the Scripture in Greek was more corrupted by them." [1] Unhappily, the common Latin text which they translated had suffered much in the course of transmission, and even the Clementine Revision, with which, at a later time, the Rhemish New Testament was harmonised, was not prepared, as Scrivener remarks, " on any intelligent principle of criticism, or furnishes us with such a text as the best manuscripts of Jerome's Vulgate supply to our hand." [2] If we examine the Rhemish version in a sympathetic spirit and with due allowance for the ecclesiastical position of its makers, we cannot but be struck by its singular freedom from dogmatic bias. What seems to the Protestant reader, familiar only with the Authorised or Revised Version, a straining of Scripture language here and there in favour of Roman Catholic dogma, is really the result of a deliberately chosen principle of literal

[1] See *Preface* to the Rhemish New Testament.
[2] See Note C, Appendix : *Origin and History of the Vulgate.*

adherence to the Latin text, and is set down in good faith. Again, though painfully loyal to the Vulgate, the Rhemists fall back for guidance on those very versions against which they polemicised so fiercely in their Preface. For instance, a critical analysis of Hebrews, chap. i, verses 1-4, shows that only two of the ninety-eight words with which they translate the passage are undoubtedly original, all the rest being found in one or other of the current versions from Wycliffe's to the Bishops' Bible. Moreover, the Greek text was consulted when the Latin failed them, as in the use of the definite article. Hence the Rhemish rendering now and again anticipates the Revision, where the Authorised Version, through carelessness, is at fault.[1] Another anticipation of the Revised Version to which the Rhemists may lay claim is its literal rendering of the " genitive of quality," which the Latin takes over from the Greek, which in turn borrows it from the Hebrew. Thus, the " gospel of the

[1] Comp. Matt. vii. 17, xxv. 30 ; Rev. vii. 13.

glory of Christ '' and '' the son of his love ''
are richer in significance than the Authorised rendering, '' the glorious gospel of
Christ '' and '' his dear son.'' The fatal
flaw, however, pervading the entire work is
the sadly inadequate conception of a translator's function with which it was undertaken. The Rhemish scholars, forgetful of
Luther's principle that '' God does not reveal
grammatical vocables but essential things,''
kept to their Latin text with bald and slavish
accuracy, reproducing its ambiguities and
obscurities and sacrificing the idiom and
spirit of the language into which they translated. Indeed, the original edition of the
Rhemish Version is an outrage on the English
tongue, crowded as it is with barbarisms,
infelicities, cacophonies, and dark sayings.
Many passages convey no meaning except to
the scholar who is able to turn them back
into Latin, and in some cases even the Latin
has lost the sense.[1] Many of these faults
have been remedied in later editions, but a

[1] See Note D, Appendix.

considerable number still remain. For example, we have:[1] " Celebrating the exequies ";[2] " nothing of that anathema shall stick to thy hand ";[3] " my chalice which inebriateth him, how goodly it is ";[4] " thou shalt not be afraid . . . of the business that walketh about in the dark, of invasion, or of the noon-day devil ";[5] " thy name is invocated upon thy city ";[6] " the Devil shall go forth before His feet ";[7] " Give us to-day our supersubstantial bread ";[8] " bearing about in our body the mortification of Jesus";[9] " let no man seduce you, willing in humanity and religion of angels ";[10] " inflameth the wheel of our nativity ";[11] " insinuating humility one to another ";[12] " every spirit that dissolveth Jesus is not of God ";[13] " the flesh of tribunes."[14] After the un-

---

[1] These passages are taken from the edition of the Douay Bible approved by Cardinal Gibbons for circulation in the United States.

[2] Gen. 1. 10.
[3] Deut. xiii. 17.
[4] Psalm xxiii. 5.
[5] Psalm xci. 6.
[6] Dan. ix. 19.

[7] Hab. iii. 5.
[8] Matt. vi. 11.
[9] II Cor. iv. 10.
[10] Col. ii. 18.

[11] James iii. 6.
[12] II Pet. v. 5.
[13] I John iv. 3.
[14] Rev. xix. 18.

learned reader has puzzled out these and others like them, he may go on to ask the meaning of " pythonic spirits," " loaves of proposition," " a rational," a " curdled mountain," " the cords of Adam." And then, what are " tamaric," " cherogrillus," " ophiomachus," " sciniph," " charadrion," " azymes "?[1]

It argues a strange blindness on the part of its creators to suppose that such a work could ever become the favourite of the English people.   As a matter of fact, though formally authorised by the ecclesiastical authorities and its worst faults removed, it has never gained the admiration of even Roman Catholic Christians, and owes its present position to the dead hand of religious conservatism that rests so heavily on the Roman Church.

In 1749, Dr. Richard Challoner, an English Roman Catholic divine, published a revision of the Rhemish New Testament, and there followed in 1750 a revision of the entire

[1] On the other hand, a touch of modernity startles us ; e.g., the reading "bankers," adopted also in the American Revision, in Matt. xxv. 27.

Douay Bible. He continued to revise and to edit his work up till the year 1777, in which he published a sixth edition of the New Testament. His revision of the Old Testament, as Cardinal Newman says, " issues in little short of a new translation." " His version," says the Cardinal, " is even nearer to the Protestant than it is to the Douay."[1] A simple inspection of almost any passage suffices to prove the greatness of Challoner's obligations to the Authorised Version. Hundreds of verses are all but identical in the two Bibles. In the New Testament, his obligations, though not so obvious as in the Old Testament, are still very great. Thus the interesting fact emerges that many dexterities and felicities of Tindale and his successors have enriched the Douay Version. So much, indeed, did Dr. Challoner lean upon King James's translators that he has unhappily appropriated, with much that is good, some elements that are no longer regarded as valid. Not infrequently he suffers him-

[1] *Tracts Theological and Ecclesiastical*, p. 416.

self to be misled into forsaking the Vulgate
and miscorrecting his Rhemish exemplar.
In scholarly circles within the Church of
Rome, there has long been a feeling that
acquiescence in the present confused state
of the Douay text is little short of a scandal.
Cardinal Newman, at the request of the
English Bishops, undertook the work of revision, but was forced to abandon the task
by obscurantist opposition. This signal
victory for ignorance and stupidity has deprived not Roman Catholics only, but the
whole of Anglo-Saxon Christendom of what
would have been a permanent enrichment of
our common Christianity, achieved as it
would have been by one of the finest religious
spirits as well as one of the greatest masters
of English in the nineteenth century.

In spite, however, of all its faults, King
James's translators found in it a rich mine
from which they drew abundantly, to the
great betterment of their own work—and this
though it was not specified in the Rules
drawn up for their guidance.   Only recently

has the full extent of their indebtedness come
to light. " Their [King James's trans-
lators] work," say the Anglo-American Revisers, " shows evident traces of the influence
of a version not specified in the Rules, the
Rhemish made from the Latin Vulgate but
by scholars conversant with the Greek
original." [1] The simple fact now appears
that there is scarcely a page of the Revised
New Testament that, through the Authorised
Version, does not bear the marks of Roman
Catholic scholarship. Dr. J. G. Carleton, an
Irish scholar, has with admirable industry
compiled no less than one hundred and thirty-
seven columns of passages in which the
Rhemish and Authorised versions, presenting either identical or similar renderings,
differ from earlier translations.[2] His results
have been tested and found singularly accurate. How far has this immense debt been
carried over to the Revised Version? For
the sake of illustration, let us select the

[1] Preface to the Revised Version of the New Testament, 1881.
[2] *The Part of Rheims in the Making of the English Bible.*

Epistle to the Philippians. It contains one hundred and four verses. Now if we compare these in the Rhemish Version with the earlier versions and with the Revised, we find that twenty-five verses or about one-fourth of the entire Epistle have been influenced by the Rhemish through the Authorised. Figures, however, do not enable us to realise with sufficient vividness our literary obligations to the exiles of Rheims. With Dr. Carleton's help, let us bring together some striking illustrations.

1. Some of our most familiar Biblical phrases—concise and weighty—are to be traced back to their literary skill and close adherence to the Vulgate. The following are examples:[1] "Why, what evil hath he done?"[2] "The one shall be taken, and the other shall be left."[3] "The son of perdition."[4] "Subverting your souls."[5]

---

[1] Comp. also Matt. xxi. 16, xxvi. 65 ; Luke i. 25, xxi. 25, xxiii. 11 ; Acts v. 33, xxviii. 15 ; Rom. i. 10, ii. 10, xii. 16 ; Heb. xii. 23.

[2] Matt. xxvii. 23.

[3] Luke xvii. 36.

[4] John xvii. 12.

[5] Acts. xv. 24.

"The goodness and severity of God."[1] "Owe no man anything."[2] "The ministry of reconciliation."[3] "To me to live is Christ, and to die is gain."[4] "Which thing is true in him and in you."[5] "The hidden manna."[6]

2. The diction of the Revisers, as of King James's translators, owes much of its stateliness and dignity to the introduction of words of Latin origin, first adopted by the Rhemists. Thus we have "malefactor" for "evil doer," "more tolerable" for "easier," "vesture" for "coat," "commandeth" for "setteth out," "translated" for "was taken away," "justified" for "made righteous," "malignity" for "evil condition."

3. Not infrequently the Revisers owe a most expressive turn to Rhemish literalisms, as, for example:[7] "Be it far from thee"[8] (*absit a te);* "God was not well pleased"[9]

---

[1] Rom. xi. 22.
[2] Rom. xiii. 8.
[3] II Cor. v. 18.
[4] Phil. i. 21.
[5] I John ii. 8.
[6] Rev. ii. 17.
[7] See also Luke x. 34, xx. 34 ; Mark x. 52.
[8] Matt. xvi. 22.
[9] I Cor. x. 5.

(non bene placitum est Deo); " to make known the mystery "[1] *(notum facere myste-rium);* " a conscience void of [Rhemish, " without "] offence "[2] *(sine offendiculo conscientiam).* Frequently the Latin gives a word for word translation of a Greek phrase, and the Latin being closely followed in the English, we have happy amendments of all preceding versions. Among many we note: " pleasures of this life "[3] for the earlier rendering, " voluptuous living "; " living water "[4] for " water of life "; " up-braideth not "[5] (suggested by Wycliffe) for " reproacheth no man "; " every weight "[6] for " all that presseth down "; " profane person "[7] for " unclean person "; " bridleth not "[8] for " refraineth not."

4. Then again, the Revisers are indebted to the excellent Greek scholarship of the Rhemists for improved renderings of single words; e.g., " punishment " for " pain "; " understanding " for " mind " ; " soul "

[1] Eph. vi. 19. [4] John iv. 10. [7] Heb. xii. 16.
[2] Acts xxiv. 16. [5] James i. 5. [8] James i. 26.
[3] Luke viii. 14. [6] Heb. xii. 1.

for " thing "; " straitened " for " pained ";
" worshippers " for " offerers "; " par-
takers " for " companions "; " reprove "
for " improve."

5. The Rhemish Version, owing to its close
dependence on the Latin, which frequently
reproduces the order of the Greek, brings out
more distinctly the force of the original by
placing the emphatic word first. Some good
results of this arrangement have found a
place in this revision. The following may be
mentioned: [1] " And his sisters, are they not
all with us? " [2] for " Are not all his sisters
with us? " " For he that hath, to him shall
be given " [3] instead of " For unto him that
hath shall it be given." " The rich he hath
sent empty away " [4] for " He hath sent away
the rich empty." " On earth peace " [5] for
" peace on earth." " This man, if he were a
prophet " [6] for " If this man were a prophet,
he."

[1] Comp. also Matt. vii. 11, xix. 6, xxii. 10 ; Mark xv. 27 ;
John ix. 39, xviii. 11 ; II Cor. x. 17 ; Eph. v. 19 : I John
ii. 12 ; Rev. ii. 7.   [2] Matt. xiii. 56.   [3] Mark iv. 25.
[4] Luke i. 53.   [5] Luke ii. 14.   [6] Luke vii. 39

6. Finally, there are renderings in the Revised Version inherited through the Authorised, which, though not exactly identical with those in the Rhemish, were evidently moulded on them :[1] " Before whose eyes Jesus Christ was openly set forth crucified "[2] was suggested by the Rhemish " Before whose eyes Jesus Christ was proscribed being crucified among you." " Godliness with contentment is great gain "[3] is an echo of the Rhemish " Piety with sufficiency is great gain." " In a figure transferred to myself "[4] was influenced by the Rhemish " transfigured unto myself."

The foregoing is an extremely inadequate indication of the generous contribution which Catholic learning has made to our English New Testament. For fuller proofs, the reader must be referred to the painstaking pages of Dr. Carleton. Study of these proofs will make clear two significant facts.

---

[1] Comp. also Luke xii. 49 ; Acts viii. 40, xiv. 23 ; I Cor. xii. 3 ; II Pet. ii. 6.

[2] Gal. iii. 1. [3] I Tim. vi. 6. [4] I Cor. iv. 6.

One is that in the English Revision the Vulgate has at last come to its own. At first understood and prized by the mass of Western Christians, then throughout the Middle Ages relegated to the background as the mediatorial functions of Church and sacraments came more and more to fill the Christian consciousness, then in the Reformation period overestimated by Roman Catholic divines and underestimated by their Reformed opponents, it has, since the seventeenth century, taken to itself a new lease of power and entered as a permanent element into the life and thought of Anglo-Saxon Christianity. " It is to the Vulgate," as has been pointed out recently, " that the English Bible owes the richness of its music and the expressive beat of its rhythm." [1] And the direct contribution of the Latin to the English, which we have just tried to describe, mediated through the Rhemish text, is only a portion of the debt, for we must remember that Tindale, Coverdale, and the makers of

[1] Gardiner, *The Bible as English Literature*, p. 302.

the Genevan version were familiar with the
phrasing and the style of the Vulgate and
could not but transfer much of these to their
translations.[1]   The other fact is that the
Roman Catholic translation, put forth pro-
fessedly as a counterblast to the reformed
versions, has gained its greatest success, not
directly but indirectly, by giving up its best
elements to enrich the offspring of its ancient
rivals.   Its own history has been a narrow
and contracted thing, but it has gained the
power of a larger life through its influence
on later versions—one of those curious little
ironies which once and again surprise the
historian of the English Bible.   It is as if, in
the task of giving the Scriptures to the people, a divinity has been at work shaping
human ends for other than men dreamed and
making a mock at our ecclesiastical and dogmatic bigotries.

[1] See Note C, Appendix.

CHAPTER VI

THE CONTRIBUTION OF THE AUTHORISED VERSION

ONE of the first acts of the theologian-king, James I., on his accession, was to summon a Conference at Hampton Court to consider the Puritan grievances as outlined in the Millenary Petition; but the iron of Scottish Calvinism had entered the soul of James and the debate was foredoomed to failure. Yet though abortive in all else, it proved the occasion, if not the cause, of one of the greatest events of modern history, the birth of that version which for well-nigh three centuries has moulded the religious diction, shaped the theology, inspired the ideals of the vast majority of English-speaking people, and still exercises its ancient sway with almost unabated prestige. It is to the leader of the Puritans, Dr. Reynolds, President of Corpus Christi College, Oxford, that the glory belongs of having dropped a seed into the royal mind, which was to burst into such flower and fruit. The demand for a new Bible formed no part of the original Puritan programme, but it happened that incidentally in the course of an address Dr. Reynolds complained of the current versions as " corrupt and not answerable to the truth of the original," and cited three mistranslations—all from the Bishops' Bible.[1] Later it would appear that the Puritans joined in the demand of their leader for a new translation on the ground that the Prayer Book Psalter contained misrendered passages.

The suggestion of a new version kindled the King's imagination. Proud of his theological learning, averse to the popular and democratic Genevan translation, enamoured of the thought of having his name identified with a Bible, which, owing to the advancing scholarship of the time, might outshine all rivals in faithfulness to the original and in literary form, he determined to let nothing

[1] Cardwell, *History of Conferences*, p. 187.

stand in the way of the great project. A
scheme of action was speedily outlined. The
revision was to be undertaken by the " best
learned in the universities "; it was then to
pass under the review of the church leaders;
and finally was to be approved by the Privy
Council and the King himself. Among the
instructions drawn up for the guidance of the
Revisers were the following: " The ordinary
Bible read in the Church, commonly called
the Bishops' Bible, to be followed and as little altered as the truth of the original will
admit." " These translations to be used
when they agree better with the text than the
Bishops' Bible: Tindale's, Matthew's, Coverdale's, Whitchurch's (the Great Bible),
Geneva." In actual practice, however, the
Revisers appear to have corrected the
Bishops' text by reference to the Hebrew and
Greek, and to have made but slight use of
the other versions named, except, as we have
seen, the Genevan. The Rhemish New Testament published by Dr. William Fulke in
parallel columns with the second edition of

the Bishops' Bible, attracted their attention, and, as has been shown, was laid under heavy contribution.

This is practically all we know about the sources of the royal version. It is by no means impossible that some day a copy of the Bishops' Bible used for purposes of correction by one or other of the Revisers will turn up. Such a discovery would dissipate much of the obscurity that at present rests upon the influences that have gone to the making of this time-honoured translation.

As to the method by which the revision was made, very little is known. " Never was a great enterprise," says Scrivener, " like the production of our Authorised Version carried out with less knowledge handed down to posterity of the labourers, their method and order of working." [1] The Revisers originally numbered fifty-four. Of these, the names of only forty-seven have been preserved. They were unquestionably among the best scholars of their day. We may note especially An-

[1] *The Authorised Edition of the English Bible*, p. 9.

drews, whose Manual of Devotions is still
a classic; Lively, " one of the best lin-
guists in the world "; Reynolds, " a very
treasury of erudition "; Killbye, " another
Apollos "; Downes, " composed of Greek and
industry "; Miles Smith, the reputed author
of the intensely interesting Preface to the
Version, " who had Hebrew at his fingers'
ends "; and Harmer, " a most noted Latin-
ist, Grecian, and Divine." They were divided into six companies, two sitting at Westminster, two at Cambridge, and two at Oxford. A portion of the Bible was allotted to
each group. As soon as any company had
finished the translation of a book, it was sent
to all the others for their suggestions; and
when the whole Bible was completed, it passed
under a final revision at the hands of six or
twelve of the leading members of the different
companies. This last review, however, appears, from internal evidence and from the
scanty time spent on it, to have been of a
very perfunctory character. Selden, the
great contemporary lawyer and scholar, in-

dicates their mode of working: " That part of the Bible was given to him who was most excellent in such a tongue. . . . And then they met together and one read the translation, the rest holding in their hands some Bible, either of the learned tongues or French, Spanish, Italian, etc. If they found any fault, they spoke; if not, he read on." [1]

The entire work occupied two years and nine months. We have but to compare this period with the ten and a half years given to the New Testament and the fourteen years given to the Old Testament in the revision of our own time to realise what an immense stride has been taken in the conception of what a Bible translation ought to be.

The Authorised Version appeared in 1611.[2] It bears on its face the signs of its genealogy; " for while it has the fulness of the Bishops' without its frequent literalisms or its repeated supplements, it has the graceful vigour

[1] *Table Talk*, Chap. V, Sect. 2.

[2] Efforts were made to standardise the version in 1638 and 1762. Our modern text is that published under the editorship of Dr. Blaney at Oxford in 1769.

of the Genevan, the quiet grandeur of the
Great Bible, the clearness of Tindale, the har-
monies of Coverdale, and the stately theological vocabulary of the Rheims.'' [1]   May we
not add that it has been reserved for the Revised Version of our time, while heir of all
these excellences, to excel in thoroughness of
scholarship and in loyalty to the sacred
originals? But considered as literature,
noble thought nobly expressed, this legacy
from the seventeenth century stands, as all
confess, supreme. Indeed, in more than one
passage, it is superior *as literature* to the
original.   Our modern Revisers would seek
to '' increase its fidelity without destroying
its charm '' and to bear witness to '' its simplicity, its dignity, its power, its happy turns
of expression, its general accuracy . . . and
the music of its cadences and the felicities of
its rhythm.'' [2]   Yet it has its defects, which,
as springing out of its historical situation,
were more a misfortune than a fault.   The

---

[1] Eadie, *The English Bible*, Vol. II, p. 226.
[2] Preface to the 1881 edition.

uncritical and corrupt character of the Greek text which was then accepted; [1] ignorance of primitive versions except the Vulgate in a debased form; imperfect acquaintance with the finer shades of Greek and Hebrew; a tendency to a too precise definition in matters of dogma; a slurring over of distinctions marked in the original; a want of uniformity in rendering; a use of diction which in the intervening centuries has become obsolete and in some instances repellent,—such are some of its undoubted weaknesses. On the other hand, it forms a mosaic of all that was best in the work of preceding translators, and this inherited wealth has been poured into the lap of our modern Revisers. But this is not all. The royal translators improved upon the

[1] The basal text used was that of the third and fourth editions of Erasmus's Greek Testament, and this in turn was based on late manuscripts. In the Old Testament the translators had the ordinary Hebrew text. They were influenced by the Vulgate and Septuagint—both in the traditional text—and by the Latin translations of the Old Testaments of the Antwerp Polyglot, and of Tremellius. They consulted also, Luther, the Zürich Bible, and the Genevan French Bible.

work of their predecessors, and many of these improvements have stood the test of time. The following may be cited.

AUTHORISED VERSION	PRECEDING VERSIONS
[1] " The kings of the earth set themselves."	" The kings of the earth stand up " or " band themselves."
[2] " Day unto day uttereth speech."	" One day telleth another " or " A day occasioneth talk thereof unto a day."
[3] " And rejoiceth as a strong man."	" Rejoiceth as a giant " or " like a mighty man."
[4] " My foot standeth in an even place."	" My foot standeth right " or " standeth upon a plain ground " or " standeth in uprightness."
[5] " Thou art my hiding-place."	" Thou art my refuge " or " Thou art a place to hide me in."
[6] " As the hart panteth after the water brooks."	" As the hart brayeth for the rivers of water " or " Like as the hart desireth the water brooks."
[7] " Deep calleth unto deep."	" One deep calleth another deep " or " One deep calleth another."
[8] " When my heart is overwhelmed."	" Is in heaviness " or " is in trouble " or " is oppressed."

[1] Ps. ii. 2.   [4] Ps. xxvi. 12.   [7] Ps. xlii. 7.
[2] Ps. xix. 2.   [5] Ps. xxxii. 7.   [8] Ps. lxi. 2.
[3] Ps. xix. 5.   [6] Ps. xlii. 1.

AUTHORISED VERSION	PRECEDING VERSIONS
1 " The pastures are clothed with flocks."	" The folds shall be full of sheep " or " The pastures are clad with sheep."
2 " The earth saw, and trembled."	" The earth saw it, and was afraid."
3 " A man of sorrows."	" A man full of " or " as is full of sorrows."
4 " We are not saved."	" We are not helped."
5 " Walk humbly with thy God."	" Walk in humbleness."
6 " For he is like a refiner's fire."	" Like a purging fire " or " like a goldsmith's fire."
7 " All things were made by him."	" Made by it."
8 " All things work together for good."	" For the best."
9 " That ye all speak the same thing, and that there be no divisions among you."	" That ye speak one thing, and that there be no dissensions among you."
10 " I determined not to know any thing among you, save Jesus Christ, and him crucified."	" I esteemed not to know any thing " or " Neither showed I myself that I knew any thing."
11 " He that is spiritual judgeth all things."	" Discerneth all things " or " discusseth all things."
12 " Stewards of the mysteries of God."	" Disposers of the secrets of God " or " Stewards of the secrets of God."

1 Ps. lxv. 13.	5 Mic. vi. 8.	9 I Cor. i. 10.
2 Ps. xcvii. 4.	6 Mal. iii. 2.	10 I Cor. ii. 2.
3 Isa. liii. 3.	7 John i. 3.	11 I Cor. ii. 15.
4 Jer. viii. 20.	8 Rom. viii. 28.	12 I Cor. iv. 1.

AUTHORISED VERSION	PRECEDING VERSION
[1] " For we are made a spectacle unto the world."	" A gazing stock unto the world."
[2] " A promise being left."	" Forsaking the promise."
[3] " The sin which doth so easily beset us."	" That hangeth so fast on us " or " that hangeth on us."
[4] " Joy unspeakable and full of glory."	" Joy unspeakable and glorious."

In these and in many other passages, the improvement is effected by a change in a word or two; [5] but, in addition, there are entire clauses and sentences, the independent work of the Authorised Revisers, which have passed unscathed the critical tests of modern scholarship. Here are a few examples : " Ye shall not surely die "; [6] " Thou hast asked a hard thing "; [7] " acquainted with grief "; [8] " lest they trample them under their feet, and turn again and rend you "; [9] " Behold a man gluttonous, and a winebibber "; [10] " and I will give rest "; [11] " And if children, then

[1] I Cor. iv. 9   [6] Gen. iii. 4.   [8] Isa. liii. 3.
[2] Heb. iv. 1.   [7] II Kings ii. 10.   [9] Matt. vii. 6.
[3] Heb. xii. 1.   [10] Matt. xi. 19.
[4] I Pet. i. 8.   [11] Matt. xi. 28.
[5] Comp. Prov. iii. 17; Isa. ix. 5; Matt. vi. 2; xxiii. 27; Luke xii. 50; Acts i. 4; Rom. xiii. 12; I Cor. vii. 35.

heirs ''; [1] '' to be conformed to the image of his Son ''; [2] '' came not with excellency of speech ''; [3] '' For whether we be beside ourselves, it is to God ''; [4] '' And be ye kind one to another ''; [5] '' godliness with contentment is great gain ''; [6] '' the blessed Potentate ''; [7] '' put him to an open shame.'' [8]

Moreover it is worth noting that many of the Authorised marginal renderings have been transferred by our Revisers to the text. Thus, for example, we have: '' One lot for Jehovah, and the other lot for *Azazel* ''; [9] '' the baptism of repentance *unto* remission of sins ''; [10] '' except they wash their hands *diligently* ''; [11] '' How long dost thou *hold us in suspense* ''; [12] '' a Son, *perfected* for evermore.'' [13]

Speaking broadly, about eight-ninths of the words of the New Testament have been taken over from the Authorised to the Revised Ver-

[1] Rom. viii. 17.
[2] Rom. viii. 29.
[3] I Cor. ii. 1.
[4] II Cor. v. 13.
[5] Eph. iv. 32.
[6] I Tim. vi. 6.
[7] I Tim. vi. 15.
[8] Heb. vi. 6.
[9] Lev. xvi. 8.
[10] Mar. i. 4.
[11] Mar. vii. 3.
[12] Heb. vii. 28.
[13] John x. 24.

sion, and the proportion is still greater in the Old Testament. As we have seen, the Authorised Version itself is a mosaic formed of nearly all that was best in previous translations, and yet the striking fact is that, amid thousands of minute changes, the Revisers have so assimilated the new elements to the old, so baptised, as it were, their work into the spirit and power of the Authorised text, that the differences are scarcely realised by the average reader.

CHAPTER VII

THE CONTRIBUTION OF THE ANGLO-AMERICAN REVISION

IF it be asked, What were the forces which have called into being a Revised Bible in our time, meant to supersede a version so rich in honour and dignity, so rooted in popular affection and associated with the great crises of Anglo-Saxon history as the Authorised? the answer is: the new scientific knowledge of the sacred tongues gained in the intervening centuries, together with the higher ideals of a translator's duty demanded by a more delicate literary conscience. The true though remote fountain-head of the Revision of the New Testament, as Bishop Ellicott, our greatest authority on matters pertaining to the Revision, reminds us, was Winer's *Grammar of the Language of the New Testament,* published in 1822.[1]   A succession of commentaries, embodying the results of the new Biblical learning and amending the Authorised Version, gradually educated the clergy, and, through them, the laity, in the necessity for some authoritative revision of what was proved to be a faulty translation.   Besides, a vast mass of manuscript unknown in King James's day is now accessible to scholars. Through the labours of a long line of students, from Griesbach to Westcott and Hort, the mass has been explored and a clue to its mazes discovered.   Our own age is especially rich in fresh finds and in new insight into old materials.   Only a few years ago was published in facsimile the *Codex Vaticanus*, the oldest and most valuable of all the manuscripts.   Its rival in age, the *Codex Sinaiticus*, was discovered in 1844, while about the same time the *Curetonian Syriac*, a version of the second century in a manuscript belong-

[1] *Addresses, etc.*, p. 8.   What Winer did for the New, Gesenius, by his Hebrew Grammar (1813), did for the Old Testament.

ing to the fifth, was brought to light. In addition, many manuscripts were collated and a more penetrating study made of the Vulgate, Septuagint, and other versions.

Gradually, as the result of this new knowledge, a movement looking toward revision began to spread. During the three years 1856-1858, no less than twenty works appeared dealing with the question.[1] Public opinion was gradually leavened, and in spite of opposition the feeling that something practical ought to be done could not be suppressed. The first step was taken in the Upper House of Convocation of Canterbury on February 10, 1870, when a proposal was carried to appoint a committee to report upon the advisableness of a revision. A few months later, a Joint Committee of both houses was elected and equipped with instructions for the task of revision and with authority to invite other Anglican and non-Anglican scholars to coöperate. This Com-

[1] Comp. Trench, *The Revision of the New Testament*, pp. 188, 189.

mittee in turn formed two Companies, one for
the Old and one for the New Testament; the
former having twenty-seven and the latter
twenty-six members, all belonging to the
United Kingdom. The actual work was begun June 22, 1870.

From the beginning of the enterprise, it
was felt that the coöperation of American
Biblical scholars was desirable and necessary.[1] What was aimed at was an international work meant for Anglo-Saxon Christendom. Hence in July, 1870, both houses of
Convocation agreed to invite the " coöperation of some American divines." Communi-
cations were opened with several scholars,
and, as Dr. Philip Schaff, himself an active
agent in the negotiations, informs us, a committee consisting of about thirty members
was formally organised on December 7, 1871,
and entered on active work on October 4,

[1] Among the American Revisers were Schaff, Thayer,
Abbot, Crosby, Hackett, Green, Chambers, Dwight, Osgood,
and Day. Among the British Revisers were Westcott, Hort,
Scrivener, Lightfoot, Ellicott, Trench, Alford, Stanley, Milligan, Moulton, Cheyne, Davidson, and Plumptre.

1872, after the first revision of the Synoptic Gospels was received from England. The work passed through five revisions before it was given to the world. Bishop Ellicott, the Chairman of the British New Testament Company, gives an interesting description of the Revisers' mode of procedure:

" The verse on which we were engaged was read by the Chairman. The first question asked was whether there was any difference of reading in the Greek text which required our consideration. If there was none, we proceeded with the second part of our work, the consideration of the rendering. If there was a reading in the Greek text that demanded our consideration, it was at once discussed and commonly in the following manner: Dr. Scrivener stated briefly the authorities, whether manuscripts, ancient versions, or patristic citations, of which details most of us were already aware. If this alteration was one for which the evidence was patently and decidedly preponderating, it was at once adopted and the work went onward. If, how-

ever, it was a case where it was doubtful
whether the evidence for the alteration *was*
thus decidedly preponderating, then a discussion, often long, interesting, and instructive,
followed. Dr. Hort, if present (and he was
seldom absent; only forty-five times out of
four hundred and seven meetings), always
took part, and finally the vote was taken and
the suggested alteration either adopted or rejected. If adopted, due note was taken by
the Secretary, and if it was thought a case for
a margin, the competing reading was therein
specified. If there was a plain difficulty of
coming to a decision and the passage was one
of real importance, the decision was not un-
commonly postponed to a subsequent meeting
and notice duly given to all the members of
the Company. (The work was then communicated to the American Company.) Our
work, with the American criticisms and suggestions, had then to undergo the second revision. The greater part of the decisions re-
lating to the text that were arrived at in the
five revisions were accepted as final, but many

were reopened at the second revision, and the critical experience of the Company, necessarily improved as it had been by the first revision, finally tested by the two-thirds majority the reopened decisions which at the first revision had been carried by simple majorities. The results of this second revision were then, in accordance with the agreement, communicated to the American Company; but in the sequel, as will be seen in the list of the final differences between ourselves and the American Company, the critical differences were but few and, so far as I can remember, of no serious importance." [1]

The guiding principle of the Revisers was that of the utmost faithfulness to the original texts. If, without trenching on this cardinal principle, they could secure rhythm or a telling phrase, they were the better pleased; but no consideration of a literary or æsthetic kind was allowed to hinder the strictest application of the canons of criticism to the fixing of the text and the correct rendering of it.

[1] *Addresses, etc.,* pp. 66-70.

Believing, moreover, that the Bible is the
charter of the Christian faith, they conceived
it to be their duty to let its voice go forth
unaffected by ecclesiastical or dogmatic prejudice. Nearly all the Revisers were Trini-
tarians; yet they reject a famous proof-text
for the doctrine of the Trinity.[1] Believing
in the inspiration and authority of the Bible,
they yet mark as later additions passages
which for ages have been accepted as authentic.[2] Nor does their belief in the divinity of
Christ lead them to spare the traditional con-
version of the eunuch or the ascription of
Godhood to the Savior in one of the Epistles.[3]

The Revisers' handling of the text to be
translated was characterised by mingled bold-
ness and caution. The autographs of an Isaiah or a Saint Paul have, of course, long since
perished beyond recall, and the question con-
fronting the Revisers was: How are we to re-
cover, if not their every word and syllable, at
least the closest approximation to them now

---

[1] I John v. 7.   [2] Mark xvi. 9-20; John vii. 53-viii. 11.
[3] Acts viii. 37; I Tim. iii. 16.

possible? As regards the Old Testament, they answered this question by simply taking the text as we have it in our ordinary Hebrew Bible. They were compelled to do so, for no known Hebrew manuscript is older than the tenth century, nor does any differ essentially from the printed text. This text is itself a recension of a still earlier one, and was settled in all probability before the Christian era. To help reach its more primitive form, we have the ancient versions, more especially the Septuagint, dating from about the second century B.C. But these versions are themselves so corrupt that reconstruction of the Hebrew on their basis was found impossible. Hence, except in a few instances, the Revisers kept to the Massoretic text, putting into the margin probable or important alternative readings. With the New Testament the case is far different. Here the Revisers were face to face with a vast number of manuscripts, some of them dating from the fourth century, with quotations from the early Fathers and with ancient versions. Out of these materials they formed a Greek text for themselves, taking each reading on its merits and assuming that the oldest manuscript, as coming nearest the originals, deserved to have a preponderating authority. For the first time in the long history of the English Bible, we have a translation of the New Testament based on all available sources—ancient manuscripts, patristic citations, and early versions. It follows that many changes, some of them startling to the ordinary reader, have been introduced. These changes have arisen mainly through a change of reading in the Greek text, the correction of wrong translations, the more exact rendering of ambiguous passages, the substitution of modern for archaic terms, the clearing up of verbal obscurities, the more uniform rendering of the same words in the original, and finally the general modernisation of the language so as to avoid phrases and words offensive to present-day taste and feeling.

As illustrations of a more correct translation, we may compare the following passages in the Authorised and in the Revised Texts:

AUTHORISED VERSION	REVISED VERSION
Hosea xiii. 14. O death, I will be thy plague; O grave, I will be thy destruction.	O death, where are thy plagues? O grave, where is thy destruction?
Isa. xlix. 6. It is a light thing that thou shouldest be my servant.	It is too light a thing that thou shouldest be my servant.
Isa. lix. 19. When the enemy shall come in like a flood, the spirit of the Lord shall lift up a standard against him.	For he shall come as a rushing stream which the breath of the Lord driveth.
Isa. lx. 5. Then thou shalt see, and flow together.	Then thou shalt see, and be lightened.
Isa. lxi. 8. I hate robbery for burnt offering: and I will direct their work in truth.	I hate robbery with iniquity, and I will give their recompense in truth.
Isa. lxiii. 6. And I will bring down their strength to the earth.	And I poured out their lifeblood on the earth.
Isa. lxiv. 4. For since the beginning of the world men have not heard, nor perceived by the ear, neither hath the eye seen, O God, beside thee, what he hath prepared for him that waiteth for him.	For from of old men have not heard, nor perceived by the ear, neither hath the eye seen a God beside thee, which worketh for him that waiteth for him.
Isa. xi. 1. And there shall come forth a rod out of the stem of Jesse, and a branch shall grow out of his roots.	And there shall come forth a shoot out of the stock of Jesse, and a branch out of his roots shall bear fruit.

AUTHORISED VERSION | REVISED VERSION

Ps. vii. 11. God judgeth the righteous, and God is angry with the wicked every day.

God is a righteous judge, yea, a God that hath indignation every day.

Ps. xviii. 5. The sorrows of hell compassed me about; the snares of death prevented me.

The cords of Sheol were round about me; the snares of death came upon me.

Turning to the New Testament, we may take the following as typical illustrations of alterations required by changes of reading in the Greek text.

AUTHORISED VERSION | REVISED VERSION

Rom. iv. 19. And being not weak in faith, he considered not his own body now dead.

And without being weakened in faith, he considered his own body now as good as dead.

Rom. viii. 1. There is therefore now no condemnation to them which are in Christ, who walk not after the flesh, but after the Spirit.

There is therefore now no condemnation to them that are in Christ Jesus.

Rom. ix. 28. For he will finish the work and cut it short in righteousness: because a short work will the Lord make upon the earth.

For the Lord will execute his word upon the earth, finishing it and cutting it short.

AUTHORISED VERSION	REVISED VERSION
Rom. xiv. 6. He that regardeth the day regardeth it unto the Lord: and he that regardeth not the day, to the Lord he doth not regard it.	He that regardeth the day, regardeth it unto the Lord.
Rom. xvi. 5. Who is the first fruits of Achaia unto Christ.	Who is the first fruits of Asia unto Christ.

As examples of changes made with a view to a more correct rendering of the text, we take the following:

AUTHORISED VERSION	REVISED VERSION
Rom. i. 4. By the resurrection from the dead.	By the resurrection of the dead
Rom. i. 5. For obedience to the faith.	Unto obedience of faith
Rom. i. 17. For therein is the righteousness of God revealed.	For therein is revealed a righteousness of God
Rom. i. 21. But became vain in their imaginations.	But became vain in their reasonings
Rom. iii. 25. Whom God hath set forth to be propitiation through faith in his blood, to declare his righteousness for the remission of sins that are past, through the forbearance of God.	Whom God set forth to be a propitiation through faith, by his blood, to show his righteousness, because of the passing over of the sins done aforetime, in the forbearance of God.

AUTHORISED VERSION

Rom. iii. 19. And all the world may become guilty before God.

Rom. iv. 20-22. He staggered not at the promise of God through unbelief; but was strong in faith, giving glory to God; and being fully persuaded, that what he had promised, he was able also to perform. And therefore it was imputed to him for righteousness.

Rom. v. 21. As sin reigned unto death.

Rom. vi. 4. Therefore we are buried with him by baptism into

Rom. vi. 5. For if we have been planted together in the likeness of his death.

Rom. vi. 17. But ye have obeyed from the heart that form of doctrine which was delivered you

Rom. vii. 4. We also are become dead to the law by the body of Christ.

Rom. ix. 1. My conscience also bearing me witness in the Holy Ghost.

Rom. x. 5. For Moses describeth the righteousness which is of the law, That

REVISED VERSION

And all the world may be brought under the judgment of God.

Yea, looking unto the promise of God, he wavered not through unbelief, but waxed strong through faith, giving glory to God, and being fully assured that, what he had promised, he was able also to perform. Wherefore also it was reckoned unto him for righteousness.

As sin reigned in death

We were buried therefore with him through baptism into death

For if we have become united with him by the likeness of his death.

We became obedient from the heart to that form of teaching whereunto ye were delivered.

We also were made dead to the law through the body of Christ.

My conscience bearing witness with me in the Holy Ghost.

For Moses writeth that the man that doeth the righteousness which is of

AUTHORISED VERSION	REVISED VERSION
the man which doeth those things shall live by them.	the law shall live thereby.
Rom. xii. 11. Not slothful in business	In diligence not slothful.
Rom. xii. 16. Condescend to men of low estate.	Condescend to things that are lowly.

For the removal of obscurities and ambiguities, note the following:

AUTHORISED VERSION	REVISED VERSION
Rom. vi. 20. For when ye were servants of sin, ye were free from righteousness.	For when ye were servants of sin, ye were free in regard to righteousness.
Rom. xii. 17. Provide things honest in the sight of all men.	Take thought for things honourable in the sight of all men.
Rom. xiv. 2. For one believeth that he may eat all things.	One man hath faith to eat all things.
1 Tim. iii. 13. For they that have used the office of a deacon well, purchase to themselves a good degree.	For they that have served well as deacons, gain to themselves a good standing
Luke xvi. 9. Make to yourselves friends of the mammon of unrighteousness.	Make to yourselves friends by means of the mammon of unrighteousness.
1 Cor. iv. 4. For I know nothing by myself.	For I know nothing against myself.

The following are examples of greater uniformity in rendering the same Greek words:

AUTHORISED VERSION	REVISED VERSION
John xv. 9-10. As the Father hath loved me, so have I loved you: continue ye in my love. If ye keep my commandments, ye shall abide in my love; even as I have kept my Father's commandments, and abide in His love.	Even as the Father hath loved me, I also have loved you; abide ye in my love. If ye keep my commandments, ye shall abide in my love: even as I have kept my Father's commandments and abide in his love.
1 Tim. ii. 7. Whereunto I am ordained a preacher and an apostle, (I speak the truth in Christ, and lie not;) a teacher of the Gentiles in faith and verity.	Whereunto I was appointed a preacher and an apostle (I speak the truth, I lie not), a teacher of the Gentiles in faith and truth.
Rom. iv. 3. It was counted unto him for righteousness. Rom. iv. 22. It was imputed to him for righteousness. Gal. iii. 6. It was accounted to him for righteousness.	It was reckoned unto him for righteousness.

About three changes in every ten verses in the Gospels and Epistles were owing to a difference in the text adopted (which, though independently arrived at, is practically identical with Westcott and Hort's) from what had been traditionally received. The total number of variations from the Authorised Version, due to all causes, is reckoned at five thousand seven hundred and eighty-eight. A small proportion of these, however, is of first-rate importance. Should any one feel disturbed by this fact, he can reassure himself with the words of Richard Bentley, the greatest critic of the eighteenth century:

" The real text of the sacred writers does not lie in any manuscript or edition, but is dispersed in them all. 'Tis competently exact in the worst manuscript now extant, nor is one article of faith or moral precept either perverted or lost in them, choose as awkwardly as you will. Make your thirty thousand variations as many more. . . Even put them into the hands of a knave or a fool; and yet, with the most sinistrous and absurd choice, he shall not extinguish the light of one chapter, or so disguise Christianity but that every feature of it will still be the same." [1]

In the interval that has elapsed since its publication, the Revision has grown in popular favour. Its undoubted faults of rhythm, its occasional pedantries, its needless changes in small points (as, for example, the snort of Job's war-horse, which is now " Aha! " instead of " Ha! ha! ") have been forgiven because of its saving virtue, faithfulness to the original texts. The ordinary reader is put in a position as near as may be to the Greek or Hebrew scholar, and in his gratitude is willing to overlook the incidental disadvantages that spring from interference with use and wont.

An agreement was entered into by the British and American Committees that the readings prepared by the American Revisers should be published as an Appendix in all copies of the English Revised Bible during a period of fourteen years. The American Re-

---

[1] Quoted in Schaff's *Companion to the Greek Testament*, p. 181.

visers undertook to discourage, during this same period, the issue of any edition other than those of the University presses. Unlike their British brethren, the surviving members of the American Committee kept together and more or less diligently engaged in the task of preparing an edition in which their Appendix, revised and enlarged, should be incorporated as a part of the text. The fruit of these additional labours appeared in 1901 in the " Standard American Edition of the Revised Version of the Bible." Thus, there are now not two Revised Versions, but two editions or recensions of one and the same Revision, an English and an American. Speaking generally, the two editions differ in a more consistent and thoroughgoing application by the Americans of the principles which guided the British Revisers. The American Revisers treat traditional terminology with but scant respect. They refuse the title of " Saints " to the Evangelists, deny the Epistle to the Hebrews to Saint Paul, and substitute " Jehovah " for " Lord " uniformly in the Old Testament. This last change they justify on the ground that " a Jewish superstition which regarded the Divine Name as too sacred to be uttered ought no longer to dominate in the English or any other version, as it fortunately does not in the numerous versions made by modern missionaries." A few archaisms retained in the English edition are modernised. The American reader is no longer puzzled by such words as " daysman," " ouches," " occupiers," " bewray," " sodden," " clouted," " chapiter," " bolled;" for he reads instead " umpire," " settings," " dealers," " make known," " boiled," " patched," " capital," and " in bloom." Nor will he be misled by the modern associations of " usury " and " temperance "; for these are displaced by " interest " and " self-control " throughout. The " arrow snake," an animal unknown to zoölogy and owing its origin to a too literal rendering of the German word " *pfeilschlange*," disappears in favour of " dartsnake." And Pharaoh is no longer compared to the fabulous dragon, but to " a great monster." Obscurities of phrase and idiom which still vex the British reader have been removed from the American edition. The term " Holy Spirit " uniformly takes the place of the now meaningless " Holy Ghost." " The fat of kidneys of wheat "[1] becomes " the finest of the wheat "; and " let us play the man "[2] is certainly more intelligible and more in accord with modern English idiom than " let us play the men." The American Revisers do not hesitate to add a few words in italics to make a passage more perspicuous; as " His disciples asked him privately, *How is it* that we could not cast it out?"[3] Or as in this verse: " The more *the prophets* called them, the more they went from them." Stylistic and grammatical purists no longer stumble at the sentence, " A fool's vexation is heavier than them both ";[4] or at the Hebraism, " Mine eye spared them from destroying them ";[5] for we have in-

[1] Deut. xxxii. 14. [3] Mark ix. 28. [5] Ezek. xx. 17.
[2] II Sam. x. 12. [4] Prov. xxvii. 3.

stead: "A fool's vexation is heavier than they both," and "Mine eye spared them, and I destroyed them not." The unlearned reader will think for the future more worthily of the householder in the parable who agreed with the labourers not for a penny but for a shilling a day. It may be doubted, however, whether the American Revisers are right in making Saint Paul compliment the Athenians on the score of their ultra-religiousness.[1] The Greek word probably means, as the English Revisers indicate, "somewhat superstitious." The usual argument, that the Apostle would not begin an address with such a discourteous remark, loses its force when we remember that in all probability we have not a verbatim report of Saint Paul's speech, but only a summary, and that it is probable we have here an ambiguous word used by the historian of the Acts and not by the Apostle. Both the American and English Companies would have done well to have modified the bluntness of their rendering: "What there-

[1] Acts xvii. 22.

fore ye worship *in ignorance,* this I set forth
unto you." [1] The Rhemists caught the exact
nuance when they rendered it: " What therefore you worship *without knowing it,* that I
preach unto you."

Finally, the American edition has improved
on the English in the external presentation
of the Bible. The running headlines, absent in
the English issue, suggest the contents of
each page, yet are free from any dogmatic
implication; the marginal references have
been still more carefully sifted; the para-
graphs are shorter and enable us better to
mark the transitions of prophetic thought and
apostolic argument; the punctuation and
typography have been minutely reviewed and
simplified. Take one illustration of the care
devoted to this last point: The American Revisers render, " So will the king desire thy
beauty; for he is thy lord." [2] The English
Revisers print " lord " with a capital, and
in so doing, impose a Christian interpretation on the letter of the Hebrew; whereas the

[1] Acts xvii. 23.   [2] Ps. xlv. 11.

American Revisers keep to the strict meaning of the text.

Taking a glance backward along the path we have travelled, we cannot but be impressed by the complex of forces, intellectual, moral, and spiritual, that have shaped the history of the English Bible. It has passed through six revisions. Version after version has been the fruit of increased knowledge and deeper insight, and each on the whole has been an improvement on its ancestors. Unwearied industry, chivalrous endeavour, pious zeal, attended its birth and helped it on its way through the centuries; nor has it lacked the consecrating touch of martyr blood. No artificial product created to serve the passions of the hour, but the vital outgrowth of the spiritual life of a great people, it has continued to live and thrive. Striking its roots into a distant past, yet not limited by it; assimilating the garnered good of centuries, yet itself presenting a still higher type of excellence,—it may confidently challenge the world to point to any existing ecclesiastical version

which approaches it in faithfulness to the
language and spirit of inspiration. This does
not mean, however, that it is the final translation for English-speaking people. That were
an idle claim in view of the growing scholarship of the time. Students are agreed that
there are many passages in the Hebrew text
as it has come down to us which are corrupt.
With a critically revised Septuagint, we may
hope that these will yet disclose their true
significance. In the New Testament, Westcott
and Hort have not said the last word. It is
well known that these scholars chiefly rely for
their text on the two oldest existing manuscripts, the *Codex Vaticanus* and the *Codex
Sinaiticus*. But recently the Western group
of manuscripts, the most famous of which is
the Græco-Latin *Codex Bezæ*, has been studied afresh in the light of the testimony borne
to it by the Old Latin and Syriac versions and
by the Fathers. Then we have the important
find by Mrs. Lewis in 1893 of the Sinaitic Syriac Gospels. A text reconstructed on the basis
of the most primitive forms of the Old Latin

and Syriac versions would take rank as predominant authorities. The Latin and Syriac versions in their earlier forms are, says a distinguished scholar, " primary authorities for determining the sacred text. Where they agree, we are listening to the *consensus* of the extreme East and the extreme West of the Roman world, speaking hardly more than a generation after the four gospels had been gathered together by the church into one collection. Such a *consensus* is never to be disregarded, even though unsupported by a single surviving Greek manuscript." [1]

Then again, the recent resurrection of a great mass of papyrus rolls from the soil of Egypt has added distinctly to our knowledge of the type of Greek in which the New Testament was written. It used to be thought that New Testament Greek was based upon the Greek of the Septuagint. We now know that the sacred writers used the common Greek of their day. Many of their phrases and con-

[1] F. C. Burkitt, in *Criticism of the New Testament* (St. Margaret's Lectures, 1902), p. 89.

structions, which were supposed to be dialectic peculiarities, have been found over and over again in the recently discovered papyri. A study of the Greek vernacular of the first century marks a new epoch in our knowledge of the grammar and language of the New Testament.[1] When along these various lines scholarship has gained assured results, we may hope that they will be made available for the great body of Christian people in a version which, while true to the venerable glories of the past, will at the same time satisfy the needs and reflect the acquisitions of the present.

[1] See Appendix, Note E.

Note A. The English Bible Before Tindale.

Note B. Tindale's Debt to the Wycliffite Versions.

Note C. On the Origin and History of the Latin Vulgate.

Note D. Wrong or Inadequate Renderings in the Vulgate.

Note E. The Greek of the New Testament.

APPENDIX

Note A.—THE ENGLISH BIBLE BEFORE TINDALE

Before Tindale, all attempts to render the Scriptures into the vernacular had been translations from the Vulgate or older Latin versions, that is, translations of a translation. From the Anglo-Saxon period we have two metrical paraphrases, that of Cædmon (*c.* 680), of which a single manuscript is preserved in the Bodleian Library, containing stories from Genesis, Exodus, and Daniel, and from the life of Christ; and that by Ælfric (Archbishop of York in 1023) containing the Pentateuch, Joshua, Judges, Kings, Esther, Job, Judith, and the Maccabees, and, in some portions, incorporating earlier translations. This collection of paraphrases by Ælfric goes by the name of " Heptateuch."

Attempts at literal translation were confined to the Psalter and the Gospels, and took the form of glosses or interlinear translations of older Latin manuscripts. Several translations of the Psalter of this type (belonging to the ninth century) are still extant (in the National Library, Paris; British Museum; Trinity College, Cambridge; Bodleian). The most distinguished translations of the Gospels are the Landisfarne Gospels, or Durham Book, in the British Museum. Here we have a Latin manuscript belonging to the seventh century and representing not the Vulgate of Jerome, but the more primitive text of the " Old Latin; " and between the lines of the manuscript there is an Anglo-Saxon translation by a priest named Aldred, who lived some three centuries later. Then we have the Rushworth gloss, or, to call it after the name of the Irish scribe, " the Gospels of MacRegol," preserved in the Bodleian. The gloss is largely transcribed from the Landisfarne Gospels. The Venerable Bede, who died about 735, is said to have translated the fourth gospel and other portions of Scripture and may even have used the Græco-Latin manuscript known as the *Codex Laudianus,* now in the Bodleian; but not even a fragment of his work is extant. We have, however, a translation of the Decalogue, of other fragments of Exodus, and of Acts, chap. xv., 23-29, which Alfred the Great prefixed to his code of laws. It is true that much of our Anglo-Saxon literature was lost through the invasion of Norseman and Dane, but enough remains to show us that the Bible held a high place in the esteem of the Anglo-Saxon church.

In the Anglo-Norman period, little was done although it appears that a Norman-French translation came into existence. Wycliffe says, in his *De Officio Pastorali,* " As lords of England have the Bible in French, so it were not against reason that they had the same in English." Metrical paraphrases, however, still appeared from time to time. Among them is to be noted especially the " Ormulum " (twelfth century), a metrical paraphrase of the stories in the Gospels and the Acts made by Ormin, an English monk of the Order of Saint Augustine; and the " Sowlehele," a metrical paraphrase of the Old and New Testaments belonging to the thirteenth century. Two prose versions of the Psalms belonging to the early part of the fourteenth century are the earliest versions of any book of Scripture done into English prose. The earlier of these two versions is by William of Shoreham, and is represented by a single manuscript in the British Museum. The other is by Richard Rolle, a chantry priest of Hampole, Doncaster. Down to about 1360, the only book of the Bible translated in its entirety was the Psalter. These fragmentary translations, however, prepared the way for the great work of Wycliffe and his followers.

In his Commentary on the Gospels, Wycliffe makes an earnest plea for a translation of the Scriptures for the ordinary people. He was himself to initiate this great work. We probably owe to him the completed translation of the New Testament. The translation of the Old Testament was largely the work of his friend, Nicholas of Hereford, although Wycliffe seems to have supplied the later books and about one-third of the Apocrypha. The whole Bible was thus done into popular speech in 1382. Wycliffe died in 1384. About 1388 his curate, John Purvey, with the aid of other friends, put out a careful revision of the whole Bible with a most interesting introduction. These Bibles were multiplied by copying and were very expensive (from $150 to $250 a copy); yet after more than 500 years, we have 170 manuscript copies— 30 of the 1382 edition, and 140 of the later revision. Purvey's Revision of the New Testament is reprinted in Bagster's Hexapla (1841). The most authoritative work on the Wycliffe versions is the critical edition in which the earlier and later ver-

sions are printed in two parallel columns, issued
by Forshall and Madden in four volumes (Oxford,
1850).

The Wycliffite origin of the versions printed by
Forshall and Madden remained unchallenged from
the fourteenth century till the year 1894, when, in
the July number of the *Dublin Review* in that
year, Father (now Abbot) F. A. Gasquet published
an article entitled *The Pre-Reformation English
Bible,* in which he propounded the theory that these
were not of Wycliffite origin but were put forth
semi-officially as an authorised Catholic translation.
Abbot Gasquet's article is reprinted in a volume
entitled *The Old English Bible and Other Essays*
(London, 1897). Accompanying the reprint is a
reply to the criticisms which had been passed upon
his theory by Mr. F. D. Mathew in the *English
Historical Review* for January, 1895, and by F. G.
Kenyon in *Our Bible and the Ancient Manuscripts*
(London, 1895). A thorough and painstaking review of the whole subject appeared in two articles
in the *Church Quarterly Review* for October, 1900,
and January, 1901. The result of the discussion is
undoubtedly to re-establish the tradition of the
Wycliffite origin of these versions. Abbot Gasquet shows much ingenuity in his argumentation,

but leaves the impression of special pleading and failure to do justice to the positive evidence in favour of the traditional belief. The contemporary evidence which points to the responsibility of Wycliffe for the origin of the translation ascribed to him remains unshaken. The testimony of John Hus ('' It is reported among the English that he [that is, Wycliffe] translated the whole Bible from Latin into English '') cannot be explained away. This report, indeed, is not exact, because we know that Hereford translated the Old Testament; but it proves that Wycliffe was regarded as responsible for the English Bible of his time. Still more cogent evidence is afforded by Knighton's Chronicle and by the condemnatory words of Archbishop Arundel, When we turn to the works of Wycliffe himself, we find many passages which advocate the spread among the English people of a Bible in the vernacular.

The really notable point which emerges in the course of the debate between Abbot Gasquet and his critics is the Abbot's admission that the versions believed to be Wycliffite are faithful renderings of the Vulgate. This fact would account for the spread of the version among those who had no Wycliffite doctrinal leanings.

Note B.—TINDALE'S DEBT TO THE WYCLIF-FITE VERSIONS

A thorough examination of Tindale's relation to the Wycliffite versions has not as yet been made. Westcott (*History*, Appendix VIII.) quotes Tindale's assertion of independence as given in the text, and adds: " The words of Tindale imply that he knew of the Wycliffite versions, and admit the supposition that he had used them, though he deliberately decided that he could not (1) ' counterfeit ' them, that is, follow their general plan as being a secondary version only; or (2) adopt their language." The same scholar finds in the Sermon on the Mount only four Wycliffite renderings which may have suggested those of Tindale. This view requires, however, some modification. It would appear from a comparison of the appended passages that Tindale used Wycliffe's language whenever it suited his purpose. On the other hand, he translates from the Greek and uses Wycliffe as he uses other helps with scholarly independence. In the passages which follow, the spelling is modernised throughout.

PURVEY'S REVISION	TINDALE
Rom. **vi.** 10: He liveth to God.	He liveth unto God.
Verse 14: For ye are not under the Law: but under grace.	Ye are not under the law, but under grace.
Verse 18: Servants of righteousness.	Servants of righteousness.
Verse 21: What fruit had ye then?	What fruit had ye then?
Rom. vii. 12: The law is holy, and the commandment is holy, just and good.	The law is holy, and the commandment holy, just and good.
Rom. vii. 2: The law of the spirit of life in Christ Jesus hath delivered me from the law of sin and death.	The law of the spirit that bringeth life through Jesus Christ, hath delivered me from the law of sin and death.
Verse 10: If Christ is in you: the body is dead from sin.	If Christ be in you, the body is dead because of sin.
Verse 13: If ye live after the flesh: ye shall die.	If ye live after the flesh, ye must die.
Verse 15: The spirit of adoption . . . in which we cry Abba Father.	The spirit of adoption whereby we cry Abba Father.
Verse 23: The first fruits of the spirit.	The first fruits of the spirit.
Verse 24: Hope that is seen, is not hope.	Hope that is seen is no hope.
Verse 26: The spirit helpeth our infirmity.	The spirit also helpeth our infirmities.
Rom. x. 14: How shall they hear without a preacher?	How shall they hear without a preacher?

PURVEY'S REVISION	TINDALE
Verse 18: The ends of the world.	The ends of the world.
Rom. ix. 3: I am left alone, and they seek my life.	I am left only, and they seek my life.
Verse 32: That he have mercy on all.	That he might have mercy on all.
Rom. xii. 11: Fervent in spirit.	Fervent in the spirit.
Verse 15: Weep with men that weep.	Weep with them that weep.
Verse 20: If thine enemy hunger, feed thou him.	If thine enemy hunger, feed him.
Rom. xiii. 1: There is no power but of God.	There is no power but of God.
Verse 9: Love thy neighbour as thyself.	Love thy neighbour as thyself.
Rom. xiv. 17: Righteousness and peace, joy in the holy ghost.	Righteousness, peace and joy in the holy ghost.
Rom. xv. 3: For Christ pleased not to himself.	For Christ pleased not himself.
Verse 8: I say, that Jesus Christ was a minister of circumcision for the truth of God.	I say that Jesus Christ was a minister of the circumcision for the truth of God.
Verse 13: And God of hope, fulfil you in all joy and peace in believing.	The God of hope fill you with all joy and peace in believing.
Verse 15: The grace that is given to me of God.	The grace that is given me of God.
Verse 21: They that heard not shall understand.	They that heard not, shall understand.
Verse 32: That I come to	That I may come unto you

PURVEY'S REVISION	TINDALE
you in joy by the will of God.	with joy, by the will of God.
Rom. xvi. 20: And God of peace tread Satan under your feet swiftly.	The God of peace tread Satan under your feet shortly.
Verse 25: By my gospel and preaching of Jesus Christ.	According to my gospel and preaching of Jesus Christ.
James i. 6: He that doubteth, is like a wave of the sea.	He that doubteth is like the waves of the sea.
Verse 8: Unstable in all his ways.	Unstable in all his ways.
Verse 12: He shall receive the crown of life.	He shall receive the crown of life.
Verse 17: Each perfect gift is from above, and cometh down from the Father of Lights.	Every perfect gift is from above, and cometh down from the Father of Light.
Verse 19: Be each man swift to hear, but slow to speak, and slow to wrath.	Let every man be swift to hear, slow to speak, and slow to wrath.
Verse 22: Doers of the word, and not hearers only.	Doers of the word and not hearers only.
James ii. 5: Rich in faith and heirs of the kingdom.	Rich in faith, and heirs of the kingdom.
Verse 17: Faith if it hath not works is dead in itself.	Faith, if it have no deeds, is dead in itself.
Verse 26: As the body without spirit is dead: so also faith without works is dead.	As the body, without the spirit is dead, even so faith without deeds is dead.
James iii. 5: The tongue	The tongue is a little mem-

PURVEY'S REVISION

is but a little member: and raiseth great things.

Verse 17: Wisdom that is from above.

Verse 18: The fruit of righteousness is sown in peace to men that make peace.

James v. 5: Ye have nourished your hearts, in the day of slaying.

Verse 12: Before all things, my brethren, do not swear neither by heaven, neither by earth, neither by whatever other oath.

Verse 14: Pray thou for him, and anoint with oil in the name of the Lord.

Verse 15: The prayer of faith shall save the sick man.

I Peter i. 21: God that raised him from death.

I Peter ii. 5: Spiritual houses and an holy priesthood to offer spiritual sacrifices acceptable to God by Jesus Christ.

Verse 17: Honour ye all men.

Verse 24: He himself bore our sins in his body on a tree.

TINDALE

ber, and boasteth great things.

Wisdom that is from above.

The fruit of righteousness is sown in peace, of them that maintain peace.

Ye have nourished your hearts, as in a day of slaughter.

Above all things, my brethren, swear not, neither by heaven, neither by earth, neither by any other oath.

Pray over him, and anoint him with oil in the name of the Lord.

The prayer of faith shall save the sick.

God that raised him from death.

A spiritual house and an holy priesthood, for to offer up spiritual sacrifice, acceptable to God by Jesus Christ.

Honour all men.

Which his own self bore our sins in his body on the tree.

PURVEY'S REVISION	TINDALE
Verse 25: Now turned to the shepherd and bishop of your souls.	Now returned unto the shepherd and bishop of your souls.
I Peter iii. 10: Constrain his tongue from evil, and his lips that they speak no guile.	Refrain his tongue from evil, and his lips that they speak not guile.
I Peter iii. 21: The putting away of filths of flesh.	The putting away of the filth of the flesh.
I Peter iv. 1: He that suffered in flesh ceased from sins.	He which suffereth in the flesh ceaseth from sin.
Verse 10: Good dispenders of manifold grace of God.	Good ministers of the manifold grace of God.
I Peter v. 6: The mighty hand of God.	The mighty hand of God.
Verse 8: Your adversary, the devil, as a roaring lion goeth about, seeking whom he shall devour.	Your adversary, the devil, as a roaring lion walketh about, seeking whom he may devour.
Verse 10: God of all grace that called you into his everlasting glory.	The God of all grace, which called you unto his eternal glory.
II Peter i. 1: Our God and Savior Jesus Christ.	Our God and Savior Jesus Christ.
II Peter ii. 17: These are wells without water.	These are wells without water.

Some of these coincidences in rendering may be accounted for by the immediate influence of the Vulgate, but the great majority show that the later translator freely used the work of the earlier.

Note C.—ON THE ORIGIN AND HISTORY OF LATIN VULGATE

The word " Vulgate " is the Latin adjective *vulgata* in the form of an English noun. It means " current " or " commonly received," some such substantive as *versio*, version, or *editio* being understood. Its Greek equivalent (*κοινή ἔκδοσις*) was applied to the Septuagint translation (250-150 B.C.). When the Old Latin version made from the Septuagint came into use, it received the title " Vulgate," which some centuries later came to be applied to Jerome's Latin Bible, consisting of a revision of the Old Latin New Testament and a translation of the Hebrew Old Testament. This last is the modern usage. When we speak of the " Vulgate " we mean the Latin Bible traditionally identified with Jerome's name, though, as we shall see, there are elements in it for which he is not responsible.

These unquestioned facts are obscured in a statement made in the Preface to Cardinal Gibbons' edition of the Douay Bible to the effect that " the Septuagint . . . which contained all the writings now found in the Douay version, as it is called, was the version used by the Saviour and His Apostles and by the Church from her infancy, and translated into Latin, known under the title of the Latin Vulgate, and ever recognised as the true version of the written Word of God." Three assumptions are made here which are groundless. (1) The Alexandrine Septuagint, which contained certain books outside the Hebrew Canon, is identified with the Septuagint current in the days of Christ in Palestine. But there are reasons for believing that the Palestinian Septuagint had practically the same books as the Hebrew Bible. (Comp. Westcott's *Bible in the Church,* p. 124.) (2) The Old Latin translation from the Septuagint is here confounded with the Latin version which goes under the name of the Latin Vulgate to-day. The two are to be distinguished; the one is the old Latin Vulgate, the other is the New Latin Vulgate. The former in the New Testament is the basis of the latter, while in the Old Testament it is displaced by a fresh translation from the Hebrew made by Jerome himself. (3) There is no proof that our Lord used the Septuagint. Whether He knew Greek is a disputed question. Modern opinion holds that he spoke Aramaic and read the Old Testament in Hebrew.

The origin of the Old Latin version is lost in obscurity. When, where, or by whom the translation was made, no man knows. It is even uncertain whether we should speak of the Old Latin version or of several independent versions. Cardinal Wiseman (*Essays on Various Subjects*) argued that there was only one Old Latin translation; but more recently Professor Sanday has maintained (*Studia Biblica*, 1885, p. 236) that there were originally " two parent stocks from which all the texts that we now have were derived by different degrees of modification." One thing is certain, or almost so, that wherever the version or versions originated, it was not at Rome. The language used there in the first two centuries was Greek. There were twelve Bishops of Rome down to the year 189 A.D. and of these only three bear Latin names. About the year 58 A.D. St. Paul writes to the Romans in Greek, and a century later Justin Martyr, who lived at Rome, wrote in the same language. (Comp. Sanday and Headlam's *Internat. Crit. Commentary on Romans* Introd.) The usual opinion till recently was that North Africa was the true home of the version; but the latest writer (comp. *Hastings' Dict.*, Art. *Old Latin Version*) decides for Antioch in Syria. What is more im-

portant to note is that the Old Latin translation,
if we may use the singular, is the daughter of the
Septuagint, itself marred by many mistranslations
and errors, which in turn were multiplied by later
copyists from whose efforts emerged the current
text. (Comp. Swete's *Introd. to the Septuagint*,
p. 103.) It was from this current text that the
unknown Wycliffe or Tindale of the second century
first translated the Bible into Latin, and of course,
later editions of his work must have been still more
corrupt. Jerome is a witness to the confusion and
diversity of the Old Latin copies in his time. " If
faith," he says, " is to be put in the Latin texts, let
them [his opponents] say in which: for there are
almost as many types of text as there are manuscripts " (*Epistle to Damasus*). Augustine speaks
of the infinite variety and number of Latin translations. He says that in early times any one who
owned a Greek codex and had some little knowledge
of both languages made bold to translate it (*De
Doctrina Christiana*, II. 14, 15). Hence according
to Augustine, *the Old Latin version which lies
behind the present Vulgate was made by private
hands, and not under ecclesiastical sanction.*

About 382 A.D. Pope Damasus commissioned
Jerome to bring some order out of chaos by revising

the Latin text of the Gospels. His qualifications
for the task were of the highest order. Earnest
piety, immense erudition, and a Latin style modelled
on the best authors marked him out as a man
providentially called to the work. He took the
Latin text most used in Italy as his basis and corrected its worst blunders by means of ancient Greek
manuscripts. For fear of giving offense to the
unlearned he left many mistakes unamended, so
that often for Jerome's own view of the correct
reading of a passage it is necessary to consult his
commentaries. For example, he rejects the Vulgate reading in Ephesians i. 6; iv. 19; Galatians v.
9. The Old Latin version belongs to the so-called
" Western " type of text, which came into existence at a very early period when copyists felt themselves at liberty to add to or subtract from their
copies. The sacred books were not yet regarded
as a trust to be kept intact for future ages, but
rather as a means of edification and devotion for
those into whose hands they might come. (See
Westcott and Hort, *The New Testament in Greek,*
Introd.) On the other hand, we have to remember
that pieces of this very primitive translation sur-
vive in the Vulgate, in spite of all corrections and
changes, and are of the highest authority. " A

comparison," says Professor Sanday, " of the oldest forms of the Syriac Version with the oldest forms of the Latin may reveal a text worthy to be put into competition with that of the famous Greek uncials " (*Criticism of the New Testament,* p. 6). Then again, Jerome corrected the Old Latin by means of Greek manuscripts, which, on the whole, were of a type represented by the text at the basis of the Anglo-American Revised Version; Codex Sinaiticus standing out as the most constant supporter of his readings. (Wordsworth and White, *Vulgate N. T.,* Pt. 1, pp. 655-672.) This explains why the Rhemish New Testament in several passages is superior to the Authorised Version and anticipates the Revised Version. (Comp. Matthew xix. 17; Mark iii. 29; Acts xvi. 7; Rev. xxii. 14.)

The revised Gospels were published in 383 A.D., the remainder of the New Testament appearing shortly afterwards.

Later, and without any ecclesiastical sanction, he undertook to translate the Old Testament, forsaking the Septuagint on which the Old Latin version was based, and rendering directly from the Hebrew. He explains why he abandoned the traditional text. " If any one is better pleased," he says, "with the edition of the Seventy, it is long since corrected by me. Yet if our friend reads carefully he will find that our version is the more intelligible, for it has not been turned sour by being poured three times over into different vessels, but has been drawn straight from the press and stored in a clean jar, and has thus preserved its own flavour " (*Letter to Summias and Fretela*, Nicene and Post-Nicene Fathers, vol. vi. p. 492). This part of his work took him fifteen years to accomplish, 390-405. Its publication drew down upon the translator a shower of abuse. Even Augustine, who was ignorant of Hebrew, criticised him at first and stood by the Septuagint, which he regarded as inspired and which he could not bear to see set aside to make way for another, even though that other was based directly on the original.

Jerome had little regard for the Apocrypha and apologised for translating Tobit and Judith. The former was in Aramaic, a language with which he was not acquainted. He had a Jew translate it into Hebrew, and he then turned the Hebrew into Latin for his amanuensis. He refused to translate Ecclesiasticus and Wisdom. It is uncertain whether he revised I and II Maccabees. These books were taken over from the Old Latin into the Vulgate. Three Latin versions of the Psalter are

connected with Jerome's name: (1) a revision of
the Old Latin version with the help of the Septuagint, called the Roman Psalter; (2) a more
thorough revision with reference to Origen's
amended text of the Septuagint, known as the
Gallican Psalter; (3) a new translation from the
Hebrew. Now it was the second of these that
eventually was incorporated in the Vulgate and
forms, in English dress, part of our modern Roman
Catholic Bible.

It follows that the Vulgate as we have it is not
a simple but a composite work. It consists of the
following:

(1) The unrevised Old Latin—the Apocrypha
     (except Tobit and Judith);
(2) The Old Latin revised—the Gospels;
(3) The Old Latin perfunctorily revised—Acts
     to Revelation;
(4) Direct translation from the Hebrew—the
     Old Testament (except the Psalms);
(5) The Old Latin revised with reference to
     Origen's revised Septuagint—the Psalms.

The Old Latin Vulgate died hard. For centuries it existed side by side with the New, and
neither could claim to be the " authentic " text.
In the sixth century Pope Gregory the Great quotes

both Vulgates indifferently " since the Apostolic See, over which by the grace of God, I preside, uses both " (Epistle prefixed to *Moralia on Job*). There is an interesting memorial of this early state of things in a manuscript called the *Codex Usserianus* I, preserved in the Library of Dublin University, belonging to the sixth or seventh century, and showing that the New Testament reached Ireland not in Jerome's revision, but in the Old Latin unrevised text. The inevitable result of the co-existence of the two Vulgates was that copyists familiar with the Old Latin often introduced readings from it into Jerome's Bible. An illustration of this kind of corruption may be seen in the double rendering of the same passage in II Samuel i. 19— (II Kings i. 18, 19): " Consider, O Israel, for them that are dead, wounded on thy high places. The illustrious of Israel are slain upon thy mountains." There is but one sentence in Hebrew of which these two sentences are double translations, the first coming from the Old Latin Vulgate, the second belonging to Jerome's Vulgate. About the seventh century the victory of the New Vulgate was assured, but by this time it had been sadly deteriorated. The causes of corruption were mainly the carelessness of copyists, their tendency

to introduce marginal notes into the body of the
text, their unconscious reminiscence of the Old
Latin, and finally, alterations for dogmatic reasons.
Vercellone in his *Authenticity of the Single Parts
of the Vulgate Version,* published at Rome in 1866
with the imprimatur of the Master of the Palace,
holds that there may be many errors of translation
even in dogmatic passages, though the dogmas based
on them are themselves free from error. (Comp.
Catholic Dictionary, p. 943.)

Berger, who is one of the greatest of our modern
authorities on the Vulgate, says: '' Dogmatic alterations, indeed, are not rare in the text of the Vulgate. . . . The doctrines most dear to the
mediæval theologians exercise all their influence
on the text of the Bible.'' (See *Histoire de la
Vulgate,* p. viii, Paris, 1893.)

Throughout the Middle Ages the history of the
Vulgate is a history of corruption, interrupted by
attempts at revision. At the end of the eighth
century, Alcuin, an English scholar, at the invita-
tion of Charlemagne, undertook a revision. His
work in course of time was gradually undone by
the errors of copyists. By the thirteenth century
chaos had come again. By command of St. Louis
of France, the doctors of the University of Paris

made a text which substantially is the basis of the modern Vulgate.

The art of printing was invented in the fifteenth century, and now a standard text could be fixed. The Council of Trent on April 8, 1546, passed the following decree—" Moreover the same sacred and holy synod—considering that no small utility may accrue to the Church of God, if it be made known which out of all the Latin editions, now in circulation, of the sacred books, is to be held as authentic —ordains and declares that the said old and Latin Vulgate edition which, by the lengthened usage of so many ages has been approved of in the Church, be in public lectures, disputations, sermons, and expositions, held as authentic: and that no one is to dare or presume to reject it under any pretext whatever." *Insuper eadem sacrosancta Synodus considerans, non parum utilitatis accedere posse ecclesiæ Dei, si ex omnibus Latinis editionibus, quæ circumferuntur, sacrorum librorum, quænam pro authentica habenda sit, innotescat; statuit et declarat ut hæc ipsa vetus et vulgata editio, quæ longo tot sæculorum usu in ipsa ecclesia probata est, in publicis lectionibus, disputationibus, prædicationibus, et expositionibus pro authentica habeatur, et ut nemo illam rejicere quovis prætextu audeat vel præsumat.*) (Comp. Schaff: *Creeds and Confessions of Christendom,* vol. ii, p. 82.)

The Council ordered that as correct an edition as possible of the Vulgate should be printed. It was nearly half a century later that an attempt was made to carry out the Council's order. Pope Sixtus V issued the first printed and authoritative text in 1590, prefaced by the famous bull " Aeternus ille," which forbade the alteration of the smallest particle on pain of the greater excommunication. (For full text of the Bull see Van Ess, *Geschichte der Vulgata,* Tübingen, 1824.) Sixtus died in August, 1590. Several short-lived Popes succeeded him. In 1592 Clement VIII came to the papal throne. It would appear that the Jesuits had never forgiven Sixtus for putting Bellarmine's book, *On the Direct Dominion of the Pope,* in the Index, and took revenge by having Clement recall the Sixtine edition to make way for a new one. The new revision was issued in 1592 with a preface by Bellarmine in which it is said that " the same Pope (Sixtus) when he was about to send it forth, perceiving that not a few errors had crept into the Holy Bible through the fault of the press, which seemed to require fresh attention, judged it wise and determined to have the whole work recalled and done over again. But as he could not carry out his design, being prevented by his death . . . at last toward the beginning of the pontificate of Clement VIII, who now governs the church universal, the work at which Sixtus aimed, with the Divine assistance, is achieved.''

Prior to the publication of this edition, Bellarmine had charged the Sixtine text not with typographical errors, but with wilful alterations whereby Sixtus brought himself and the whole church into serious peril'' se totamque ecclesiam discrimini commiserit Sixtus V ''—and had recommended that the book should be recalled, revised, and then sent forth under the name of Sixtus with a preface putting the blame on the printers. (See the original document, quoted by Van Ess, pp. 290, 291.) Owing to this unworthy prevarication, Bellarmine at a later date was denied canonisation. (See Van Ess, pp. 298-318.) Two modern scholars, Bishop Wordsworth and Mr. White, have examined the Sixtine edition and pronounce it excellently printed for the time. (*Vulgate N. T.*, p. 724.) They found only twelve misprints in the New Testament. Clement's text differs from that of Sixtus in about three thousand places (Bukentop,

Lux de Luce, Bk. III, 1710), and remains to the present day the authorised official Bible of the Roman Catholic Church. It is usually issued under the names of Sixtus and Clement and thus the fact is disguised that there were really two revisions. The Douay divines had translated the whole Bible (though the New Testament only was issued) prior to the appearance of the Clementine Vulgate. Before issuing their Old Testament they brought their version into accord with the official text (see Preface to Douay Old Testament). The New Testament was revised with reference to that text by Dr. Challoner and others.

Is the Clementine revision an accurate representation of Jerome's work? " One thing is certain," says Dr. Scrivener, " that neither the Sixtine nor the Clementine edition (the latter of which retains its place of paramount authority in the Roman Church) was prepared on any intelligent principles of criticism or furnishes us with such a text as the best manuscripts of Jerome's Vulgate supply to our hand " (*Introd. to the Criticism of the N. T.,* p. 352, 3d edition).

The decree of the Council of Trent calling for the editing of as correct a copy of the Vulgate as possible seems at last in our own time about to be realised. The late Pope Leo XIII created a commission for the study of the Scriptures, but little real work was done. On April 30, 1907, Cardinal Rampolla, President of the Commission, entrusted the work of revision of the Vulgate to the Benedictines, and appointed Abbot Gasquet, the well-known English scholar and historian, as head of the committee. The collaboration of ecclesiastics and laymen, Catholics and non-Catholics, is invited. Some idea of the gigantic nature of the task is given when it is said that about 26,000 MSS. must be collated and arranged as a preliminary to the task of translation. Benedictines will be sent to the libraries of the entire civilised world for the purpose of consulting MSS. The expense will be borne in part by the Vatican, but in part also by Roman Catholic Christendom. The first part of the task proper will be the reconstruction, as far as possible, of the text of Jerome. This reconstructed text will be the foundation of the revision. The next step will be to discover how far Jerome himself was correct. Probably the Psalms will be undertaken first. Abbot Gasquet will probably issue first a critical edition of the Psalms in Jerome's three versions, printed in parallel columns, together with probably the old " Itala " version.

When this work is finished, it will be one of the greatest monuments of Christian scholarship and industry our age has known. (See article on *Revision of the Vulgate*, by S. Cortesi. in *Pall Mall Magazine*, March, 1908.)

Note D.—WRONG OR INADEQUATE RENDERINGS IN THE VULGATE

THE Douay Bible labours under all the weaknesses and crudities of its basal text. Its very loyalty to the Vulgate has proved its undoing. This is especially conspicuous in the Psalter, which demands more fidelity, perhaps, than any other book in the Old Testament, to the spirit of the original. Nevertheless, the painful fact must be stated that this is the worst rendered and most obscure part of the entire volume. The meaning has to be described, dimly enough, through three translations, Hebrew to Greek, Greek to Latin, Latin to English, and the English is harsh, crabbed, pedantic, wholly unfitted to voice the aspirations, the joys and sorrows of the soul. The Douay Psalter is thus, in addition to its own inadequacies, heir to the faults and blunders of two translations, the Septuagint and the Old Latin. There are, for example, interpolations in the Septuagint, taken over by the Old Latin and Englished in the Douay. (See Psa. vii. 12; xii. 6; xiii. 3; from *their throat* to *before their eyes* [inserted by a Christian hand in the Septuagint from Rom. iii. 13-18]; xxxii. 10; cxxxi. 5, Douay trans. and notation.)

Again, the Greek translators blundered as to the meaning of Hebrew words and phrases and the Old Latin followed them blindly. For example, Psalm lxxxvii. 16, we have " in labours " when the Hebrew is " ready to die "; and lix. 10, " Moab is the pot of my hope " for the Hebrew, " Moab is my wash-pot." (Comp. Psa. lix. 6; cxix. 127; cxl. 5, Douay.)

A curious illustration of the unhappy servility of the Old Latin to the Septuagint is seen in Psalm cxxxi. 15 (Douay): " Blessing I will bless her widow," where for " widow " the American version reads " provision." The Hebrew word (*tsidah*) means both " prey " and " provision," and the Septuagint choosing the former significa- tion rendered it *theran*, and *theran* was uninten- tionally or otherwise altered to *cheran*, which means "widow."

In the course of transcription many corruptions

crept into the Greek text. Notes made in the
margin were by later copyists deemed part of the
original, so that we have in many places
" doublets," that is, two renderings of one and the
same expression. For example, Psalm xxviii. 1
reads in the Douay: " Bring to the Lord, O ye
children of God: bring to the Lord the offspring
of rams." The Hebrew phrase has an ambiguous
sound (*bene elim*) between " children of God "
and " offspring of rams." One of the renderings
was an alternative marginal reading in the Septuagint, but eventually got into the text and so passed
into the Old Latin. We have thus in the Vulgate
a double translation of the same words.

Sometimes the fine imagery of the original is
utterly spoiled. In Psalm xxiii. 7 (Douay) we
have the rendering: " Lift up your gates, O ye
princes " where the Revised Version has: " Lift
up your heads, O ye gates." The striking image
in the Hebrew which personifies the great gates of
Zion and calls upon them to lift up their heads
that the King of glory may enter with erect mien,
is ruined and there is substituted for it the gro-
tesque idea of princes carrying gates. " The gates
which raised their heads were turned into the heads
which raised their gates." This blunder is repro-

duced in a picture in St. Alban's Psalter of a prince carrying a couple of gates to a figure representing Christ.   (See *Jewish Quarterly Review*, vol. xi, p. 164.)

The Septuagint translators unfortunately allowed themselves to take liberties with the sacred text such as the softening of expressions apparently out of harmony with the character of the subject of which they were used.   A striking illustration is supplied by the words addressed to Moses concerning Aaron: " And thou shalt be to him as God." The Septuagint, followed by the Vulgate, tones down the phrase to: " Thou shalt be to him in *those things that pertain to God*," Exodus iv. 16.   (Comp. Exod. v. 3; Psa. viii. 5; xvii. 15; xc. 2; xcvii. 7; cxxxviii. 1, R.V. notation.)

In the same way Jerome is misled by other Greek translations.   One curious blunder he owes to the version of Aquila, a non-Christian Jew of the second century before Christ.   We read in the Douay Bible: " And they saw that the face of Moses when he came out *was horned*," Exodus xxxiv. 35; where the Revisers have: " And the children of Israel saw the face of Moses that the skin of Moses' face shone."   Strangely enough, this old mistranslation has been consecrated

in the horns of Moses chiselled by the hand of
Michael Angelo on the tomb of Pope Julius II at
Rome. (See *Jewish Quarterly Review,* vol. xi, p.
165.) (For Rabbinical legends incorporated by
Jerome in the Vulgate and retained in the Douay
version, comp. I Sam. v. 9; Isa. xxxiii. 17.) But
the great Latin Father has native as well as inherited faults. His chief weakness is a tendency
to impose a more distinctly Messianic reference on
certain passages than they can justly bear in the
original, thus obscuring the true order of revelation. Jacob in his deathbed address to his sons is
made to predict the coming of the Messiah: " The
sceptre shall not be taken away from Judah . . .
till he come that is to be sent and he shall be the
expectation of all nations," Genesis xlix. 10. But
the Hebrew does not yield this meaning: it is much
more vague and mysterious. " The sceptre shall
not depart from Judah . . . until Shiloh come
and unto him shall the obedience of the people be."

Similarly he finds an allusion to the grave of
Christ in the words of Isaiah: " His sepulchre shall
be glorious," though the Hebrew bears no such
meaning: " His resting-place shall be glorious "
(xi. 10.) His unhistorical way of viewing revelation misleads him into an unwarrantable tamper-

ing with the text. Take for example a passage which runs in the Hebrew as translated by the Revisers thus: " Send ye the lambs for the ruler of the land, from Sela to the wilderness unto the mount of the daughter of Zion," Isaiah xvi. 1. (Comp. II Kings iii. 4.) The prophet calls on Moab, afraid of the Assyrians, to send a tribute of lambs to the King of Judah the ruler of the land of Edom, so that the Moabites may claim his protection against the invader. For this historical reference, Jerome substitutes, without the slightest justification, a prediction of Him who should be revealed as the Lamb of God: " Send forth, O Lord, the Lamb, the ruler of the earth, from Petra of the desert to the mount of the daughter of Zion." To take a final illustration we have the strange rendering: " Let us put wood on his bread," instead of which the Revised Bible reads " Let us destroy the tree with the fruit (margin, *bread*) thereof," Jeremiah xi. 19. The words form a proverb, and they are uttered by the prophet's enemies as an expression of their hatred, meaning, " Let us utterly make an end of him." But Jerome finds in the saying an allusion to Christ, of whom Jeremiah was a type, and in his Commentary refers " bread " to Christ's body the

Bread from Heaven, and " wood " to the Cross.
Hence the translation. (Compare for other examples, Job xix. 25-27 ; Isaiah xii. 8 ; xlv. 8 ; Daniel
x. 24-27. See Gigot, *General Introduction,* pp.
323-325.)

Note E.—THE GREEK OF THE NEW TESTAMENT

" The Greek papyri of Egypt are in themselves
nothing novel; but their importance for the historical study of the language did not begin to be
realised until, within the last decade or so, the
explorers began to enrich us with an output of
treasure which has been perpetually fruitful in
surprises. The attention of the classical world has
been busy with the lost treatise of Aristotle and the
new poets Bacchylides and Herodas, while theologians everywhere have eagerly discussed new
' Sayings of Jesus.' But even these last must
yield in importance to the spoil which has been
gathered from the wills, official reports, private
letters, petitions, accounts, and other trivial sur-
vivals from the rubbish-heaps of antiquity. They
were studied by a young investigator of genius, at

that time known only by one small treatise on the
Pauline formula ἐν Χριστῷ, which, to those who read
it now, shows abundantly the powers that were to
achieve such splendid pioneer work within three
or four years. Deissmann's ' Bibelstudien ' appeared in 1895, his ' Neue Bibelstudien ' in 1897.
It is needless to describe how these lexical researches in the papyri and the later inscriptions
proved that hundreds of words, hitherto assumed
to be ' Biblical,'—technical words, as it were,
called into existence or minted afresh by the language of Jewish religion,—were in reality normal
first-century spoken Greek, excluded from literature
by the nice canons of Atticising taste. Professor
Deissmann dealt but briefly with the grammatical
features of this newly-discovered Greek; but no one
charged with the duty of editing a Grammar of NT
Greek could read his work without seeing that a
systematic grammatical study in this field was the
indispensable equipment for such a task. In that
conviction the present writer set himself to the
study of the collections which have poured with be-
wildering rapidity from the busy workshops of Oxford and Berlin, and others, only less conspicuous.
The lexical gleanings after Deissmann which these
researches have produced, almost entirely in docu-

ments published since his books were written, have
enabled me to confirm his conclusions from independent investigation.

" The new linguistic facts now in evidence show
with startling clearness that we have at last before
us the language in which the apostles and evangelists wrote. The papyri exhibit in their writers
a variety of literary education even wider than that
observable in the New Testament, and we can match
each sacred author with documents that in respect
of Greek stand on about the same plane. The conclusion is that ' Biblical ' Greek, except where it is
translation Greek, was simply the vernacular of
daily life. Men who aspired to literary fame wrote
in an artifical dialect, a would-be revival of the
language of Athens in her prime, much as educated
Greeks of the present day profess to do. The NT
writers had little idea that they were writing literature. The Holy Ghost spoke absolutely in the
language of the people, as we might surely have expected He would. The writings inspired of Him
were those:

> " Which he may read that binds the sheaf,
> Or builds the house, or digs the grave;
> Or those wild eyes that watch the wave,
> In roarings round the coral reef."

The very grammar and dictionary cry out against men who would allow the Scriptures to appear in any other form than that ' understanded of the people.' '' J. H. Moulton, *A Grammar of New Testament Greek,* Vol. I. pp. 3-5 (Edinburgh, 1906).

BIBLIOGRAPHY

I. THE ENGLISH VERSIONS FROM TINDALE'S TO THE ANGLO-AMERICAN REVISED VERSION

TINDALE'S BIBLE

The New Testament. First edit., 1525; second, 1534.
Reprint in Bagster's Hexapla, *Lond.*, 1841. Facsimile
reprint, edited by F. Fry, *Bristol*, 1862.

The Five Books of Moses. First edit., 1530. Reprint,
edited by J. I. Mombert, *N. Y. & Lond.*, 1884.

Works of William Tyndale, edited by H. Walter, for
the Parker Society, 3 vols., *Cambridge*, 1848-50.

Whole Works of W. Tyndale *et al.*, edited by J. Daye.
Lond., 1573.

J. Foxe. Acts and Monuments. First edit., folio, *Lond.*,
1562; ninth, 3 vols., 1684. Many times reprinted and
abridged. Seymour's abridgment, *Lond.*, 1838.

D. Wilkins. Concilia Magnæ Britanniæ et Hiberniæ,
vols. III & IV, *Lond.*, 1787.

J. Strype. Ecclesiastical Memorials. First edit., 3 vols., *Lond.,* 1721; others, *Lond.,* 1816, *Oxford,* 1822. Memorials of Archbishop Cranmer. Folio, 1694; *Oxford,* 1812, 1840; *Lond.,* 1848, 1853.

T. Fuller. The Church History of Britain until the year 1648. *Lond.,* 1655, 1837, 1842; *Oxford,* 1845.

G. Joy. An Apology made to satisfy W. Tindale. 1535. Reprint in English Scholar's Library, *Birmingham,* 1882.

J. A. Froude. History of England, vol. III. *Lond.,* 1856-70.

F. Fry. A Bibliographical Description of the editions of the N. T., Tyndale's version in English, etc. *Lond.,* 1878.

J. Gairdner. The English Church in the Sixteenth Century. *Lond.,* 1902.

J. L. Cheney. The Sources of Tindale's N. T. (Dissertation for degree of Ph.D. at Leipzig.) *Halle,* 1893.

J. R. Slater. The Sources of Tyndale's version of the Pentateuch (Ph.D. thesis). *Chicago,* 1906.

The Athenæum. May 2, 1885. Tindale's Hebrew Scholarship. Jan. 8, Aug. 12, Sept. 14, 1889, Tindale's New Testament.

The Atlantic Monthly. Vol. 85. The Bible, the Father of English Prose Style.

Good Words. Vol. 26, p. 1329. The First English Bible. *J. L. Porter.*

COVERDALE'S BIBLE

Original editions, 1535-50.   Reprint in Bagster's
Hexapla, 1838.

Writings and Translations of Miles Coverdale, edited by
G. Pearson, for the Parker Society.   *Cambridge,* 1841.

Remains of Miles Coverdale, edited by G. Pearson, for
the Percy Society.   *Cambridge,* 1846.

B. Botfield.   Some Account of the First [Coverdale's]
English Bible, 1870.

MATTHEW'S BIBLE

First edit., 1537.   (Made by J. Rogers from Tindale's
and Coverdale's translations.)

J. L. Chester.   John Rogers, the Compiler of the First
Authorised English Bible.   *Lond.,* 1861.

State Papers, Henry VIII, vol. I.

See also *Foxe, Strype,* etc., *under* Tindale.

GREAT BIBLE

Original editions, 1539, 1540, 1541.

Reprint of the Psalter of 1539, *Lond.,* 1894.

F. Fry.   A Description of the Great Bible, 1539, and
of Cranmer's Bible, 1540-41.   *Lond.,* 1865.

See also references under Tindale and Coverdale.

GENEVAN BIBLE

First Genevan New Testament (Whittingham's). *Geneva,*
1557. Reprint in Bagster's Hexapla, 1842.
The Genevan Bible. *Geneva,* 1560.

Original Letters on the English Reformation. Vol. II.
Cambridge, 1847.
Life of W. Whittingham. Camden Miscellany, vol. VI.
Westminster, 1870. Reprinted in Lorimer's Life of
John Knox, *Lond.,* 1875.
W. F. Hook. Lives of the Archbishops of Canterbury,
vol. IX. *Lond.,* 1872.

The Bibliographer. (Lond.) July, Sept., Nov., 1882;
Mar., July, 1883, *N. Pocock.*

BISHOPS' BIBLE

Folio editions, 1568, 1572; quartos, 1569, 1570. Second
edition reprinted by Fulke, 1589.

W. Fulke. A Defence of the Sincere and True Trans-
lations of the Holy Scriptures into the English
Tongue. *Lond.,* 1583, 1633. Reprinted for the
Parker Society, *Cambridge,* 1843.
Correspondence of Matthew Parker (originals in the
Record Office, London). Published by the Parker
Society, *Cambridge,* 1853.

H. J. Todd. A Vindication of our Authorised Translation and Translators of the Bible and of preceding English versions. *Lond.,* 1819.

The Bibliographer. Jan.-April, 1882. *N. Pocock.*

The Athenæum. Feb. 25, 1888; Aug. 15, 1903. *N. Pocock.*

RHEIMS-DOUAY BIBLE

Rhemish New Testament. First edit., *Rheims,* 1582. Challoner's Revised N. T., 1749, etc.

Douay Bible (with Rhemish version of N. T.). First edit., 2 vols., *Douai,* 1609-1610. Challoner's Revised O. T., 1750, etc. Modern versions are based on Challoner.

Reprint of the text of the Douay and Bishops' Bibles, edited by W. Fulke, 1589.

R. Parsons. A Brief Discourse contayning certain reasons why Catholiques Refuse to goe to Church. *Douai,* 1580.

Rainold. Refutation of sundry Reprehensions. *Paris,* 1583.

W. Whitaker. Answer to Rainold's Refutation. *Lond.,* 1583.

W. Fulke. Confutation of the Rhemish Testament. Reprinted, *N. Y.,* 1834.

T. Cartwright. The Answers to the Preface of the Rhemish Testament. *Edin.,* 1602.

F. Bacon. Of the Pacification of the Church (1604). In Works, edited by B. Montague, vol. VII, p. 81. *Lond.,* 1827.

A. Possevino. Apparatus Sacer. 1608.

T. Cartwright. A Confutation of the Rhemish translation, glosses and annotations in the N. T. *Leyden,* 1618.

Pitt. Relationes Historicæ de Rebus Anglicis. *Paris,* 1619.

A. à Wood. Athenæ Oxonienses. *Lond.,* 1691.

Bibliotheca Literaria : being a collection of inscriptions, etc. *Lond.,* 1723.

Dodd. Church History of England, 3 vols. Vol. II. *Brussels,* 1737.

A. Geddes. Prospectus of a new translation of the Holy Bible. *Glasgow,* 1786.

Catholicus (pseud.). Notes on the Preface of the Rhemish Testament. *Dublin,* 1813.

Hamilton. Observations on the Present State of the Roman Catholic English Bible. (Addressed to Archbishop Murray of Dublin.) *Dublin,* 1825.
A Second Letter to the Most Reverend Dr. Murray. *Dublin,* 1826.

N. P. S. Wiseman. Catholic Versions of Scripture. In Essays on Various Subjects, 3 vols. Vol. I. *Lond.,* 1853. (Originally appeared in *The Dublin Review,* April, 1837.)

G. D. Notice sur une traduction anglaise de l'Ecriture Sainte, désignée ordinairement Bible de Douai et Nouveau Testament de Reims. 1849.

Archbishop Murray's Douay and Rhemish Bible Examined. *Lond.*, 1850.

J. Dixon. A General Introduction to the Sacred Scriptures. Amer. edit., *Baltimore,* 1853.

H. Cotton. Rhemes and Doway: an attempt to show what has been done by Roman Catholics for the diffusion of the Holy Scriptures in English. *Oxford,* 1855.

J. G. Shea. A Bibliographical Account of Catholic Bibles, etc., printed in the U. S. *N. Y.,* 1859.

J. H. Newman. The Rheims and Douay Version of Holy Scripture. In " Tracts Theological and Ecclesiastical." *Lond.,* 1874. (Originally appeared in *The Rambler,* July, 1859.)

E. B. O'Callaghan. A List of Editions of the Holy Scriptures and parts thereof printed in America previous to 1860. *Albany,* 1861.

Concilii Plenarii Baltimorensis II Acta et Decreta. 1866.

Records of English Catholics under Penal Laws. Vol. I. The Douay Diaries, with Introductions. Vol. II. Letters and Memorials of Cardinal Allen. *Lond.,* 1878.

Concilii Plenarii Baltimorensis III Acta et Decreta. 1880.

Father Clark. The Pope and the Bible. *Lond.,* 1889.

T. Donnelly (Father Donnelly). Rome and the Bible. *Lond.,* 1897.

J. S. Vaughan. Popular Use of the Bible encouraged by the Catholic Church. *Lond.,* 1897.

C. F. B. Allnatt. The Bible and the Reformation. *Lond.,* 1897.

J. G. Carleton. The Part of Rheims in the Making of the English Bible. *Oxford,* 1902. (See *Amer. J. of Theology,* below.)

Gigot. General Introduction to the Study of the Scriptures. *N. Y.,* 1903.

———

Dictionary of National Biography, *Lond.,* 1885—. Notices of the translators and revisers of the Rheims-Douay Version.

A Catholic Dictionary. Sixth edit. *Lond.,* 1903. The Douay Bible.

———

The British Critic (Lond.). Sept., 1817. Troy's Bible.

The Dublin Review. See Wiseman above.

The Rambler. See Newman above.

The Quarterly Review (Rom. Cath.). Oct., 1861. pp. 19 ff.

The Month: à Catholic Magazine. (Lond.) June, July, 1897. Our English Catholic Bible.

American Journal of Theology. July, 1903. Review of Carleton's Part of Rheims in the Making of the English Bible.

AUTHORISED VERSION

Original edition, 1611. Reprinted in Bagster's Hexapla, 1841.

Critical edition with Translators' Address to the Reader,

in the Variorum Teachers' edition of the Holy Bible, *Lond.*, 1880.

W. Barlow. Sum and Substance of the Conference at Hampton Court, Jan. 14, 1603. Reprinted in The Phenix, *Lond.*, 1707, and in Cardwell's History of Conferences, *Oxford*, 1840.

Report of Delegates to the Synod of Dort in 1618. Extract reprinted in Scrivener's Authorised Edition. See below.

R. Gell. An Essay toward the Amendment of the last English Translation of the Bible. *Lond.*, 1659.

G. Burnet. History of the Reformation of the Church of England. First edit., 1681. Pocock's edition. Vol. V. *Oxford*, 1865.

T. Fuller. Church History of Britain. Book X, sec. 3. First edit., 1755; others, *Lond.*, 1842, 1845.

J. Selden. Table Talk. Chap. V, sec. 2. First edit., *Lond.*, 1689; edition by S. H. Reynolds, *Oxford*, 1892.

A. Geddes. Prospectus of a new translation of the Holy Bible. *Glasgow*, 1786.
Letter to the Lord Bishop of London. *Lond.*, 1789.
Address on the Publication of the N. T. *Lond.*, 1793.

D. Wilkins. Concilia Magnæ Britanniæ et Hiberniæ. Vol. IV. p. 432. *Lond.*, 1787.

G. Wakefield. A New Translation of those parts only of the New Testament which are wrongly translated in our common version. *Lond.*, 1789.

W. H. Roberts. Corrections of Various Passages in

the English Version of the Old Testament. *Lond.*, 1794.

Notes upon Mistranslations, or the Present Translation of the New Testament Examined. *Boston,* 1804. (71 pp.)

J. P. Smith. Revision of the N. T. *Boston,* 1810. See *Eclectic Review* below.

J. W. Whitaker. An Historical and Critical Enquiry into the Interpretation of the Hebrew Scriptures. *Cambridge,* 1819-20.

E. Cardwell. Documentary Annals, 1546-1716. 2 vols. *Oxford,* 1839.

A. W. McClure. The Translators Revised. *N. Y.,* 1853.

Hall. Companion to the Authorised Version of the New Testament. *Lond.,* 1857.

R. C. Trench. On the Authorised Version of the New Testament. *Lond. & N. Y.,* 1858.

F. H. A. Scrivener. Cambridge Paragraph Bible (with introduction). *Cambridge,* 1873.
Authorised Edition of the English Bible, 1611. *Cambridge,* 1884.

F. Field. Notes on Select Passages of the Greek Testament, with references to recent English versions. In Otium Norvicense. Vol. III, 1864. Reprinted as Notes on the Translation of the New Testament, edited by A. M. Knight. *Cambridge,* 1899.

William Aldis Wright. The Authorised Version of the English Bible, 5 vols. *Cambridge,* 1909.

The Eclectic Review. Jan.-April, 1809. New Versions

of the N. T. *J. P. Smith.* Separate reprint, *Boston,* 1810.

Bibliotheca Sacra. Jan., 1859, Vol. 16. Early Editions of the Authorised Version. *E. W. Gilman.*

The Historical Magazine. Dec., 1861. The Early Editions of King James's Bible. *J. Lenox.* Reprinted, *N. Y.,* 1861.

The Quarterly Review. July, 1872, Vol. 133, p. 1476. The Revision of the English Bible.

REVISED VERSION

New Testament (with preface). *Oxford* and *Cambridge,* 1881.

Old Testament (with preface). *Oxford* and *Cambridge,* 1884.

American Standard Edition of the Revised Bible. *N. Y.,* 1891.

A. Dewes. A Plea for a new translation of the Scriptures. *Lond.,* 1866.

P. Schaff. The Revision of the English Version of the Holy Scriptures by co-operative committees of British and American scholars. *N. Y.,* 1873.

P. Schaff. The Revision of the English Version of the New Testament by Trench, Lightfoot, and Ellicott. *N. Y.,* 1873.

Anglo-American Bible Revision Committee. By Members of the Committee. Published by the Amer. Sund. School Union. *N. Y.,* 1879.

C. J. Ellicott. Address to the Upper House of the Convocation of Canterbury, May 17, 1881.

G. V. Smith. A Reviser on the New Revision. *Lond.,* 1881.

E. W. B. Nicholson. Our New Testament. *Lond.,* 1881.

G. Salmon. The Revision of the New Testament. *Dublin,* etc., 1881.

A. Roberts. Companion to the Revised Version of the New Testament. With supplement by a member of the committee (P. Schaff). *N. Y.,* 1881.

Lee. Co-operative Revision of the New Testament. *N. Y.,* 1882.

W. G. Humphrey. A Commentary on the Revised Version of the New Testament. *Lond.,* 1882.

B. H. Kennedy. Ely Lectures on the Revised Version of the New Testament. *Lond.,* 1882.

J. A. Thoms. A Complete Concordance to the Revised Version of the New Testament, embracing the marginal readings of the English revisers as well as those of the Amer. committee. *Lond.,* 1882.

E. Beckett. Should the New Testament be Revised? (Unfavourable to revision.) *Lond.,* 1882.

F. C. Cook. The Revised Version of the First Three Gospels. *Lond.,* 1882.

W. A. Osborne. The Revised Version of the New Testament. *Lond.,* 1882.

C. J. Ellicott and *E. Palmer.* The Revisers and the Greek Text of the New Testament. By two members of the N. T. Committee. *Lond.,* 1882.

C. J. Vaughan. Authorised or Revised? *Lond.,* 1882.

W. W. Simpkins. The English Version of the New Testament compared with King James's Translation. *Pella, Iowa,* 1882. (43 pp.)

T. W. Burgon. The Revision Revised. (Three Articles reprinted from *The Quarterly Review.*) *Lond.,* 1883.

D. R. Goodwin. Notes on the Late Revision of the N. T. Version. *N. Y.,* 1883.

Lindsay. Criticisms on certain passages in the Anglican Version of the New Testament as revised.

T. W. Chambers. Companion to the Revised Old Testament. 1886.

P. Schaff. A Companion to the Greek Testament and the English versions. Third edition, 1888.

B. F. Westcott. Some Lessons of the Revised Version of the New Testament. Second edition, *Lond.,* 1897. See *Expositor,* below.

A Documentary History of the work of the American Committee on Revision. *N. Y.,* 1885.

An Historical Account of the work of the American Committee on Revision of the Authorised English Version of the Bible. (Based on the preceding collection of documents and drawn up by Bishop Lee, Dr. Dwight, and Dr. Day.) *N. Y.,* 1885.

C. J. Ellicott. Addresses on the Revised Version of Holy Scripture. *Lond.,* 1891.

J. B. Lightfoot. On a Fresh Revision of the English New Testament. Third edit. *Lond.,* 1891.

J. Jacobs. Studies in Biblical Archæology. (Chap. VII—The Revised Old Testament.) *N. Y.,* 1894.

London Times. July 20, 1881. Posthumous article by *Dean Stanley.*

Contemporary Review. July, 1881. *J. J. S. Perowne.*

American Journal of Philology. 1881-82. *C. Short.*

The Expositor. Sec. Ser., Vol. II. *W. Sanday.*

Bibliotheca Sacra. Vols. 59 and 60. On the American Revised Version. *H. M. Whitney.*

Catholic Presbyterian. Vol. V, p. 401. The Revised Version of the New Testament. *P. Schaff.*

North American Review. Vol. 88, 1859, Bible Revision. *L. E. Smith.* Vol. 132, p. 427. The Revised Version. *P. Schaff.*

Edinburgh Review. July, 1865. Vol. 129, pp. 103 ff. Revision of the English Bible.

New Englander. May, 1879. Vol. 38. The Revision of the Authorised English Version of the New Testament. *T. Dwight.* Reprinted, *New Haven,* 1879.

Quarterly Review. 1882. New Testament Revision: the new English Version. *T. W. Burgon.*

The Expositor. 1887. *C. J. Ellicott.*

II. GENERAL HISTORICAL INFORMATION

Many of the following works contain chapters or sections on the special versions of Part. I.

Smith's Dictionary of the Bible. 1877.

Encyclopædia Britannica. 1878. Art., English Bible.

New International Encyclopædia. 1902.

Hastings's Dictionary of the Bible. Extra volume. 1904.

New Schaff-Herzog Encyclopædia of Religious Knowledge. 1908. Vol. II. Art., Bible Versions.

Hastings's Dictionary of the Bible (Single volume). 1909.

Bibliotheca Literaria. Vol. IV, pp. 1-23, an essay upon the English Translations of the Bible. 1723.

A. Johnson. An Historical Account of the Several English Translations of the Bible. 1730. Reprinted in R. Watson's Collection of Theological Tracts. Vol. III. 1791.

W. Newcome. An Historical View of the English Biblical Translations. *Dublin,* 1792.

R. Grier. Answer to Ward's Errata of the English Bible. *Lond.,* 1812.

J. Lewis. History of the Several Translations of the Holy Bible into English. 1731, 1739, 1818.

S. P. Tregelles. The English Hexapla. 1841.

T. Ward. Errata of the Protestant Bible. New edition, *Dublin,* 1841; *N. Y.,* 1844.

C. Anderson. Annals of the English Bible. 2 vols. 1845-1862.

G. Offor. MS. Notes in Anderson's Annals, British Museum.

H. Cotton. List of Editions of the Bible and Parts thereof, 1805-1850. Sec. edit., *Oxford,* 1852.

M. Stuart. The Bible and the Versions of the Bible. 1856.

Bibliotheca Sacra. April, 1858. Vol. 151, p. 261. English Translations of the Bible.

F. Fry. Description of the Great Bible and the Editions of the Authorised Version. 1865.

W. F. Kirby. Gleanings from Many Fields, or the Early Days of our English Bible. 1870.

T. Walden. Our English Bible and its Ancestors. 1871.

W. J. Loftie. A Century of Bibles, 1611-1711. *Lond.,* 1872.

J. Eadie. The English Bible. 2 vols. *Lond.,* 1876.

H. Stevens. The History of the Oxford Caxton Memorial Bible. *Lond.,* 1878.

W. F. Moulton. The History of The English Bible. *Lond.,* 1878.

P. Schaff. Bible Revision. 1879.

T. J. Conant. The English Bible. *N. Y.,* 1856. Reprint as " Popular History of the Translations of the Holy Scriptures." 1881.

S. Newth. Lectures on Bible Revision. 1881.

B. Condit. History of the English Bible. *N. Y.,* 1882.

Woolcombe. The English Bible and its Versions. 1882.

F. Bowen. A Layman's Study of the English Bible in its Literary and Secular aspects. *N. Y.,* 1886.

W. T. Dobson. History of the Bassandyne Bible, the first printed in Scotland. *Edin.,* 1887.

J. R. Dore. Old Bibles. *Lond.,* 1888.

A. Edgar. Bibles of England. *Paisley, etc.* 1889.

J. P. Smyth. Old Documents and the New Bible. 1890.

J. Wright. Early Bibles of America. 1892.

R. Lovett. The Printed English Bible, 1525-1885. 1891. Reprint, Present Day Primers, No. 2. *Chicago & Lond.,* 1894.

R. T. Talbot. Our Bible and how It has Come to Us. 1894.

F. G. Kenyon. Our Bible and the Ancient Manuscripts. 1896.

W. Milligan. The English Bible. 1896.

Harper's Magazine. Vol. 104. The Pedigree of the English Bible.

J. A. Clapperton. Pitfalls in Bible English. *Lond.,* 1899.

W. B. Thomson. The History of the English Bible. Bible Class Primers. *Edin., etc.* (1900).

R. G. Moulton. The Literary Study of the Bible. 1895. The Modern Reader's Bible. (Edited by R. G. Moulton.) *N. Y.,* 1898. A Short Introduction to the Literature of the Bible. *Boston,* 1901.

H. W. Hoare. The Evolution of the English Bible. *Lond.,* 1901, 1902.

W. Rosenau. Hebraisms in the Authorised Version of the Bible. *Baltimore,* 1903.

B. F. Westcott. General View of the History of the English Bible. *Lond.,* 1868, 1872, 1905.

W. J. Heaton. Our Own English Bible. 1905.

J. H. Gardiner. The Bible as English Literature. *N. Y.,* 1906.

J. I. Mombert. English Versions of the Bible: a Handbook. *Lond.,* 1883, 1896, 1907.

I. M. Price. The Ancestry of our English Bible. Sec. Edit. *Phil.,* 1907.

J. Gairdner. Lollardy and the Reformation in England. 2 vols. *Lond.,* 1908.

Protestant and Roman Catholic Bibles Compared. Three Gould prize essays edited by M. W. Jacobus. *New York,* 1908.

Henslow. The Vulgate, the Source of False Doctrine. *Lond.,* 1909.

Quarterly Review. April, 1870. Vol. 128, p. 301. The English Bible.

J. R. Harris. Sidelights on New Testament Research. *Lond.,* 1909.

INDEX

Allen, William, 63-67
American Edition of Revised Version, its virtues, 119-122; criticism of, 121
American Revisers, The, 103
Andrews, 91
Anglo-American Revision, The, 100-126
Anglo-American Revisers, their impartiality, 107
Antwerp Polyglot, 94
Augustine, St., 146
Authorised Version, 87-97, 116

Bellamine, Cardinal, 154-155
Berger, 152
Bentley, Richard, 146
Beza, 71
Bible, The, Tindale's version, Coverdale's version, 27-38; Matthew's version, 35; Public use of, 41; Genevan version, 40-53, 54-85; Revised Version, 19, 25-26, 33-34, 63, 73, 87-91, 107; The Great Bible, 36-39, 44, 55-58, 93; Authorised Version, 46, 48, 87-97, 116; Bishops' Bible, 55-62, 73-88; Roman Catholic version, 63-86; Rhemish version, 34, 70-72, 76, 80-83, 89; Anglo-American Revision, 100-126

Bible, the Great, 36-39, 44, 55-58, 93
Bishop's Bible, 55-62, 73-88
Blaney, Dr., 92, *footnote*
Brastow, Richard, 69-70
British Revisers, 103
Burkett, F. C., 125

Calvin, 42
Carleton, Dr. J. G., 79-81, 84
Challoner, Richard, 76-77
Church Quarterly Review, 136
Clementine Vulgate, 155-156
Colet, 2
Coverdale, Miles, personality, 28; style, 29; studies, 30; his translation, 31-33; compared with Tindale's, 33-34, 37; with Matthew's text, 35
Cromwell, Thomas, 28

Damasus, Pope, 147
Dante, 5
Douay Diaries, 64-68; Appendix. *Note C. passim*
Downes, 91

Eadie, Dr., 93
Edward VI., 40
Elizabeth, Queen, 30, 54-63
Ellicott, Bishop, 100-104

English Bible, the, its history and organic growth, 123
Erasmus, 2, 3, 13, 15, 40, 94

Foxe, 1
Fulke, William, Dr., 89

Gairdner, James, 28
Gardiner, S. H., 85; *footnote*
Gardiner, Bishop, 28
Gasquet, Abbot, 135-136, 157
Genevan version, the, 40-54, 86-93
Gigot, Francis E., *footnote*, 20
Gilby, Anthony, 43
Gregory, the Great (Pope), 141
Griesbach, 101

Hampton Court Conference, 87
Hus, 136

Jerome, St., 71-72

Kilbye, 91
King James I., 77-79, 87, 101
Knox, John, 42-44

Lamb, Charles, 58
Latimer, Hugh, 27
Laurence, Giles, 55
Lewis, Mrs., 124
Lively, 91
Luther, 14, 74, 94

Martin, Gregory, 67-69
Matthew, Thomas, 35

More, Sir Thomas, 11-12, 22
Münster, Sebastian, 36

Newman, Cardinal, 77-78

O'Connell, Daniel, 70
Old Latin Version, 134-151

Parker, Archbishop, 55
Parsons, Robert, 67, *footnote*
Purvey, John, 134-135

Reuchlin, 22
Revised Version, the, 19, 25-26, 33-34, 63, 73, 87-91, 107
Reynolds, Dr., 87-88
Rhemish Version, the, and the Rhemists, 34, 70-72, 76, 80-84, 89
Rogers, John, 7
Roman Catholic version, 63-86

Saintsbury, 1
Sampson, Thomas, 41, 44
Sanday, 145-148
Schall, Dr. Philip, 104, 116, *footnote*
Scrivener, 90-156
Seeden, 92
Semitic Idioms, 25
Shakespeare, 46
Smith, Miles, 91

Tindale, William, 1; published works, 5; the translation, 7-16; qualifications, 10, 20; style, 11, 12; scholarship, 20-26; his debt to Wycliffe, Appendix Note B

Tremellius, 94
Trench, Archbishop, 102,
    footnote
Trent, Council of, 153-154

Vendeville, Dr., 64
Vercellone, 152
Vulgate, 6, 14, 31-34, 71-85,
    94; Appendix, C and D

Westcott and Hort, their
    edition of the Greek N. T.,
    115, 124, 147

Westcott on Tindale, 13, 26
Whitchurch's Bible, 91
Whittingham, William, 41-
    42
Wiseman, Cardinal, 145
Wordsworth   and   White,
    their edition of the Vul-
    gate N. T., 15, 148, 156
Wood, Anthony, 69
Worthington, Thomas, 68
Wycliffe, 3, 36, Notes A
    and B

Zelyffe, 14